THE SEA

STOI
1000–2000AD

John Odam
in association with
Brigid Chapman

S.B. Publications

By the same author
Bygone Seaford

To my wife Jenny – for suffering me through two books and keeping me sane when frustrated by the behaviour of my poor old word processor.

First published in 1999 by S. B. Publications,
c/o 19 Grove Road, Seaford, East Sussex BN25 1TP

ISBN 1 85770 123 2

Designed and typeset by CGB, Lewes
Printed by Adland Print Group Ltd
Unit 11, Bellingham Trading Estate, Franthorne Way, London SE6 3BX

CONTENTS

Page

Acknowledgements   4
Introduction
1 SEAFORD THE SEAPORT c1000–1440   7
2 CINQUE PORT POWERS, from 1544   14
3 POCKET BOROUGH POLITICS c1600–1800   17
4 ELECTING A BAILIFF – AND A MUTINY
  AT BLATCHINGTON c1780-1832   25
5 FLOODS AND SEA DEFENCES 1800-1900   36
6 A FASHIONABLE WATERING PLACE? c1800-1870   45
7 NOT SO HAPPY HOLIDAYS c1870-1900   57
8 IN SICKNESS AND IN HEALTH c1900-1939   66
9 PUTTING ON THE RITZ – AND
  ANOTHER WAR c1940-1960   81
10 A SEA CHANGE c1960–   92

Appendix I Days of danger 1747-1998   103
Appendix II Schools in Seaford   112
Appendix III Local information   114
Bibliography   116
Index   117

ABOUT THE AUTHOR

John Odam FRIBA FRSA Assoc. CSD, is an architect who ran a London practice until disabled in a motor accident in 1966. In 1968 he did some lecturing at the Inchbald School of Design for occupational therapy and after nine months became its Director of Design for the next twelve years. He moved to Seaford in 1982 and dis- covered the Seaford Museum of Local History in 1984. He has been vice chairman of the museum for most of the last twelve years, represents it on the Sussex Museums' Group and served as the group's chairman in 1987-89.

ACKNOWLEDGEMENTS

The author wishes to express his deepest thanks to the Seaford Museum of Local History, just for being there and for providing research material for a substantial part of this book. Also to Brian Taylor for his willing help in finding negatives in the museum's archives and making prints; Dennis and Mary Crutch for many facts about the Beame Lands; Roger Hayes for his advice about the private schools; Joan Astell for some of the political intrigues of the eighteenth century, Ordnance Survey for permission to reproduce the maps; Seaford's Town Manager, now its Town Clerk, Leonard Fisher; and the staff of the County Records Office at Lewes and the many other kind people who have given generously of their time and expertise.

PICTURE CREDITS

The author and publisher wish to thank Redmore Church for kindly giving permission for the reproduction of his Seaford poster on the back cover; also Fotobox, Seaford for permission to reproduce the photographs on pages 92, 94, 98 and 111 and Francis Smitheman for permission to reproduce a photograph of his original oil painting of the *St Paul* on page 104.

Front cover: Seaford from Seaford Head.
(Photo: Nigel Trigwell)

Back cover: a rare railway advertising poster for Seaford, published by the London, Brighton and South Coast Railway Company, c.1920s

INTRODUCTION

Seaford has survived one thousand years of recorded history, but sometimes only just. When the Normans invaded they found fishing village with a good harbour protected by a shingle bank and doing a brisk maritime trade in wheat and wines. It became part of the Cinque Ports Federation and among the privileges granted to it from 1298 for supplying ships for Crown service was the right to send two members to Parliament.

The Black Death, constant attacks by French marauders and the shifting of the shingle bank brought about the town's first period of decline and by 1400 it had lost its Parliamentary franchise and most of its population. But by 1544 it had recovered enough to receive a charter of incorporation as a Cinque Port from Henry VIII and the following year give the French raiders a bloody nose in a battle at the Buckle.

From 1641 it was once more represented in the seat of power and it became one of the most distinguished of rotten boroughs, benefiting from being in the pocket of the Duke of Newcastle and the influential Pelham family who 'arranged' for it to elect William Pitt the Elder, later Lord Chatham; the great statesman, George Canning and other notable ministers of state..

It lost its franchise in 1832; another of its battles with the sea in the great storm of 1875; and its borough status in 1886.

Seaford, once it had a railway station, tried hard but failed to become a fashionable seaside resort like its neighbours along the coast. It was more successful when the recuperative properties of its fine sea air were made known by the developers of the day and the first convalescent hospital in the country opened there in 1861. Others followed and hot on their heels came a host of private boarding schools, attracted by the low land values which allowed them to build big houses with acres of playing fields.

The second World War brought about another change of fortunes. Once the austerity years were over the building boom started and the population, estimated at 10,310 in 1949, was soon over the 20,000 mark. As one after another the private schools closed down, the land they occupied was developed with new estates of houses that attracted the rich and not-so-rich retired, and young upwardly mobile families with jobs that enabled them to afford whatever the mortgage might be. More shops opened, more local business were set up together with all the peripherals of social progress such as a community college, leisure centre, art gallery and museum.

Seaford has, its seems, at last become what its position and topography intended it to be – a town by the sea (but still with a weather eye on it) in which it is a pleasure to live, work, rest and play.

John Odam
Seaford
May 1999

The 13th century Undercroft now restored and part of the Crypt
Gallery opened in 1994.

1

SEAFORD THE SEAPORT
c1000-1440

An Iron Age hill fort on Seaford Head, some traces of Roman occupation and a few Saxon references to 'Sefordt', are the only indications of the existence of any settlement in the locality before the Norman Conquest.

In the far distant past the Ouse flowed sluggishly into the sea across the width of Seaford Bay and at high tide waves would break against the rising ground of what was to become Bishopstone and lap along the line taken to Denton by the present A259 road. Later climate changes caused winds and tides to create a great shingle bank which ran from west to east right across the bay, far further out than the present shoreline. It blocked off the river's direct entry to the sea, diverting its flow to the east until it met the solid obstruction of Seaford Head.

The Norman invaders were quick to appreciate the strategic and commercial importance of the large lagoon-like natural harbour that had formed on the landward side of the shingle bank. It became part of the network of south east coast ports – the principal ones were Dover, Hastings, Romney, Hythe and Sandwich – that in return for certain constitutional and commercial privileges, provided ships and men for service to the Crown. Seaford, like Rye and Winchelsea, was a 'limb' of Hastings, and, like them, was later accorded the title of 'Ancient Town and Port.'

It was one of the busiest of the Channel ports in terms of trade, paying more in respect of customs duty on imports and exports between 1203 and 1205 than Rye, Pevensey or Shoreham. And its merchants were careful to see that they only paid what was due. In 1263 they took the bailiffs

This conjectural plan is based on the contours of the coastline in the Middle Ages

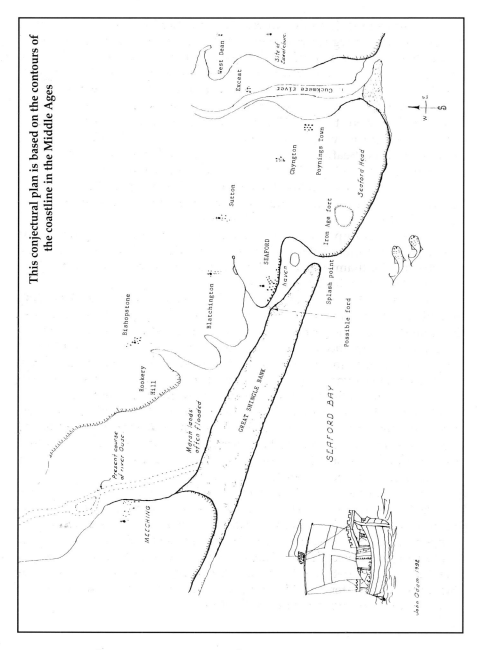

West Dean

Site of
Exceatchurch.

Exceat

Cuckmere river

Poynings Town

Chyngton

Seaford Head

Sutton

Iron Age fort

SEAFORD

haven

Bishopstone

Blatchington

Splash point

Possible ford

Rookery Hill

Present course
of river Ouse

Marsh lands
often flooded

GREAT SHINGLE BANK

SEAFORD BAY

MEECHING

John Odam 1992

of their liege lord, John de Warren, seventh Lord of Lewes, to court at Shoreham for charging fourpence duty on every grain bin shipped through Seaford and succeeded in getting the amount reduced to the original penny a bin. However, wool rather than grain was the commodity that was shipped out in the greatest quantity. There were sixteen wool merchants listed in the port at the end of the thirteenth century – considerably more than at Chichester, Shoreham or Winchelsea – and unlike these ports, where exporters used any available ships, Seaford merchants used Seaford ships. In 1293 they beat the records of all the other ports, exporting 184fi sacks of Downland wool. That does not sound a lot, but a sack of wool takes up much more space than a sack of grain of equivalent weight and nine sacks was the average amount carried with other cargo in the ships of those days.

As wool was shipped out, wines came in and Seaford appears in the exchequer accounts of the period, together with such ports as Ipswich, Chichester, Southampton and Bristol, as paying the duty of two shillings per cask levied by the 'King's Butler'.

However it was Seaford's military rather than its cargo handling activities that brought it a royal visitor. King John, having lost Normandy and other French possessions, needed a navy to protect his English kingdom and looked to the five (Cinque) ports and their 'limbs' to provide him with fifty seven ships manned by 1,195 men and boys, for fifteen days a year unpaid royal service. He made a number of tours through Kent and Sussex in the later years of his reign, not only for the hunting but to bind the ports closer to the Crown by granting new charters extending their powers and privileges in return for more ships and longer service. It was on his last tour in 1216 that he came to Seaford from Canterbury on May 23 to check on his ships and the next day moved on to Bramber where he stayed for three days.

To get there he would have either to ride six miles inland to Lewes where there was a bridge across the Ouse – or ford the river to the east of Seaford at low tide. The possible site of such a ford is indicated on the conjectural map, (see facing page 8), and no doubt it was at this point that a ferry, first recorded in 1326, operated. The existence of this ferry is mentioned again between 1369 and 1385 when it was used to convey the Bishop of Chichester and his carriages, men and farm beasts across the Ouse on the way either to or from Canterbury.

The turreted fore and aft 'castles' of the early Middle Ages (ship A) had, by the fourteenth century (ships B) become more a part of the design of the hull than an attachment to it. More masts, more sails and a more rounded and built up hull (ships C)
increased the sea worthiness and fighting capabilities of fifteenth century vessels.

The design of the ships that lay at anchor in Seaford's harbour or made their ponderous way out to ply their trade around the coast or over to the Continent changed over the years as a consequence of the dual role they were required to fill. The hulls became rounder and of deeper draught, offering greater stability and more cargo space. As a concession to their military role, in the days before gunpowder, a wooden battlemented 'forecastle' was constructed at the bow and an 'aftercastle' at the stern from which archers could fire flights of arrows in attack or defence as they did from castles on the land.

Seaford, like the other Cinque Ports, had to supply ships to ferry troops across the Channel in the early stages of the Hundred Years' War, a series of occasional conflicts which started when the male line of the Capet dynasty died out in 1337 and Edward III laid claim to the French throne. He did so by right of his mother Isabella, daughter of Philip IV, arguing that although by Salic law a woman could not rule the descendants of a woman, if in the direct line, could succeed. This claim was pursued by successive English monarchs with varying degrees of enthusiasm until 1453, by which time only the Channel Islands and the town of Calais remained in English hands.

Throughout the period of the dispute, and for some time after it, the French made hit and run raids on the Channel ports, usually sweeping in from the sea under cover of darkness and setting fire to houses and barns and making off on the next tide with whatever they could carry in the way of stores and livestock. They met little resistance in 1378 when they fired the rectory at Sutton, for by then Seaford as a flourishing seaport, its harbour entrance guarded by a fort on the clifftop, was in a state of serious decline. The sea that had created the harbour was in process of destroying it. Westerly gales swept sand and shingle over the protective bank into the harbour and narrowed the river mouth so that the flow of the outgoing tides was reduced, forcing the Ouse to deposit its natural scourings of soil in the valley instead of pushing it out to sea. As a result the estuary was becoming a marshy flood plain, useless for raising crops, cattle or sheep.

Nature had other nastiness in store, not only for the Sussex coast but for the whole of England at the end of 1348. The Black Death, a terrible plague from Asia which had devastated Europe, was brought across the Channel by flea-infested black rats, and within a year it had halved this island's population of some four million. Four fifths of the inhabitants of the nearby parish of Exceat died of the disease and the few that survived moved away – Exceat was later merged with the parish of West Dean and ceased to exist as anything but a name and a mark on a map.

A similar fate befell the manors of Sutton and Chyngton, which were merged with Seaford in 1509. Their decline started earlier and ended later. In 1296, with fifty six names on the Subsidy Roll, they formed a thriving agricultural community with peasant cottages, small farmhouses, barns and crofts gathered round the parish church of St Leonards, and village green. In 1340, nearly four decades before its rectory was fired by the French, Sutton, like a number of other Sussex villages, reported in a Poll Tax return that many of its fields were untilled because the inhabitants were too poor – and the weather had been too bad. By 1428 the situation was even worse. In a return covering parishes with less than ten households Sutton was shown to have no inhabitants.

Seaford had also suffered. By 1358, according to a precept of Edward III, 'the inhabitants had become so few as a result of the pestilence and calamities of war that they can no longer pay their taxes or defend themselves against their enemies'. They said much the same in 1380, again blaming the raids by the French, and adding:

'as many as 200 burgesses were dwelling here before the said destruction.'

By the turn of century the town could not even afford to pay the expenses of its two members of parliament, William Chitting and Robert Harry. Since 1298, when the oddly-named Geoffry Cuckou and William Holby represented it, Seaford had been the only subordinate Cinque Ports with the right to send two members to Parliament and, in consequence, was accorded precedence over all but the main ports in the Guestling or council of the federation. It lost that distinction when it surrendered its franchise in 1400 and did not recover it until 1641, when once again elections were held.

Although it had no voice at the seat of power Seaford did get some government help in the mid fifteenth century. Two local landowners, Robert, Lord Poynings and Sir John Pelham, were appointed Commissioners and given the task of renewing and repairing the shingle bank. Lord Poynings' remedy was to resite the town, rather than repair the damage done to it by the sea, and he set about building what appears

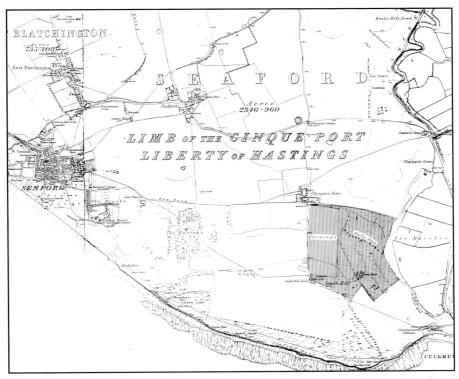

The shaded area on this 1873/4 Ordnance Survey map indicates the site of the short-lived settlement of Poynings Town and Walls Brow.

on old maps as Poynings Town and Walls Brow on the Downs overlooking the estuary of the Cuckmere. However the new settlement, like the one it was intended to replace, was attacked, presumably by French marauders, and totally destroyed. An archeological survey in the 1820s revealed old walls and foundations bearing marks of destruction by fire.

2

CINQUE PORT POWERS
1544–1885

Seaford's importance as a Cinque Port was advanced under the Tudors in spite of the deterioration of its harbour. In 1544 it was granted a charter of incorporation by Henry VIII who was keen to encourage the occupants to make up the deficiency in the number of ships supplied by the head port of Hastings. The charter itself gives the reason why:

> 'The town of Hastings . . . by conflagrations there often committed by such our enemies, not only of lands and tenements, but also of the inhabitants, there so reduced to waste, destruction and poverty, that the said town, or the barons and honest men of the same, are not sufficient to find their part of shipping to us and our heirs as they ought of their own strength. . .

It confirms Seaford's status as a Town, Borough and Parish with its own bailiff and court 'to hear and determine according to the laws of England and the Cinque Ports all please and plaints'; gives the inhabitants immunity from tolls and customs and freedom from the jurisdiction of, or services on the juries of other courts in the land; and bestows upon it 'every privilege and immunity' including powers to:

i) punish foreigners as well as natives for theft and to have a pillory and a ducking stool

ii) raise mounds or banks in any man's land against breaches of the sea

iii) appropriate to their own use all lost goods and wandering cattle if not claimed within a year and a day

iv) convert to their own use such goods as they found floating in the sea, those thrown out of ships in a storm and those driven ashore when no wreck or ship was to be seen, and

v) their barons to have the sole privilege of supporting the canopy over the head of the monarch at a coronation.

The year after they had received these powers the people of Seaford again faced a French attack. A fleet commanded by the High Admiral of France, Claude d'Annabant, sailed into Seaford Bay after unsuccessful raids on Brighthelmston and Meeching, but this time they met with fierce resistance. A force led by Sir Nicholas Pelham, pictured right, whose family's arms bear an augmentation of honour in the form of a buckle granted to Sir John de Pelham for the capture of King John of France at the battle of Poitiers – the buckle being from the king's surrendered sword – was waiting for them.

A bloody battle ensued and the French withdrew to their ships, leaving some hundred corpses on the beach in an area known to this day as the Buckle. The occasion is also commemorated by some punning lines on Sir Nicholas' tomb in St Michael's church, Lewes.

His valours proofe his manly vertues prayse
Cannot be marshall'd in this narrow roome
His brave exploit in great King Henry's days
Among the worthye hath a worthier tombe:
What time the French thought to have sack't SEA-FOORD,
This Pelham did RE-*pel'em* back aboord!

However, by this time Seaford was a port in status and name only. The movement of the shingle bank over the centuries had narrowed the harbour entrance to the width of a single vessel and often closed it totally in strong south westerly gales. Various royal commission had suggested building new wooden piers and breakwaters and reinforcing the existing ones but the work was never carried out. The high cost of timber was the cause, and the Sussex iron industry, with its voracious appetite for charcoal, was the culprit according to a royal commission of 1548 which states:

> 'If the iron mills be suffered to continue there will not only be such scantie of timber that there will not be to build in the parts near them neither houses, watermills or windmills, bridges, sluices, ships and boats for the King's majesty: beside the lack of timber that will be for the making of gunstocks, wheels. . .also the aforesaid towns which are at a daily charge of making piers and jutties for the defences of shall not be able to have in the country nigh by reason of the iron mills timber sufficient to maintain their peers and jutties. . . for whereas in the fifteen years last past upon the Downs a load of wood was commonly bought and sold at 14d and now by reason of the mills and furnaces every load is enhanced to 2s 8d and 3s and this the iron mills and furnaces do damnify and hurt thye inhabitants of the aforesaid towns'.

All efforts to maintain the access to the harbour by digging out the shingle that was being forced into it came to an end when the Ouse made a new mouth for itself by breaking through the bank between the present Tide Mills and the old Buckle Inn. When this occurred is not known. The earliest reference to a 'New Haven' is in a list of ports and harbours of 1565 which, incidentally, makes no mention of Seaford. Another return of that year makes the pitiful state of the once proud Cinque Port at the end of the sixteenth century quite clear:

> '. . . there is neither haven, creeks, nor other landing place, save upon the stone beach only, and it hath householders 38, fishermen 7, and one boat of two tons named *Nell*. . .'

❐ ❐ ❐

3

PEOPLE AND POLITICS
c1600 -1800

Seaford has a near perfect set of Town Records dating from 1562. and they show that the weather and the wars caused little variation in the daily lives – and misdemeanors – of the inhabitants in the sixteenth and seventeenth centuries. Year after year, publicans were brought before the jurats for selling beer below the proper measure; householders for throwing dead dogs, dead hogs, stones and rubbish onto the streets; and citizens for sheep stealing, practising witchcraft and looting ships wrecked in the bay. Seaford men committed the latter offence so frequently and with such efficiency that they were known as 'cormorants' or 'shags'. Even the vicar, the Reverend Robert Hyde, was suspected of acquiring £300 from a wreck in the early seventeenth century.

The penalties meted out for these offences were mostly fines and the occasional whipping or ducking. There were exceptions. In 1583 Nicholas Gabriell, a shepherd of Chingtinge (Chyngton) was sentenced to be hanged for the theft of six sheep. He claimed benefit of clergy and, having proved that he could read from the Bible, had his sentence reduced to branding on the left hand. Had he been hanged it would have been from the 'pillory tree' on the site of Old Tree Inn in the High Street.

The more recent the records the more revealing they are about the people and the town in which they lived. The Elphick family, lords of the manor of Sutton, held the office of bailiff thirty four times between 1566 and 1691. Another family of note was the Gratwickes, lords of the manor of Seaford from 1603, but their social behaviour left a lot to be desired. Sir William Gratwicke faced a fine of 2d in 1606 if he failed to

The town hall and courthouse in the 1920s when, during repairs, a stone arch was discovered below ground level. The arch (bottom left) now frames the wrought iron Coronation gate to the Crouch Gardens in East Street.

remove before Michaelmas the stones he had thrown into the highway. Lady Margery Gratwicke was taken to court for failing to remove the 'sulledge and rubbedge lying in the street against her new house'. This was Place House or Seaford Place in Broad Street and it bore the date 1603 and the initials G on its eastern front. W M

Lady Gratwicke, had she deigned to do so, would have appeared before the jurats in the courthouse adjoining the town hall in South Street. By then,

18

although only forty one years old, it was in need of repair and Seaford had also to pay its share of the cost of the confirmation of the general Charter of the Cinque Ports. To meet these expenses a rate of £65 was levied on the inhabitants and the money must have been raised, for there is no further mention of the debt. In fact entries in the records begin to indicate a revival in the town's fortunes. A Muster Roll of 1619 shows the Trained Band was well equipped. It had:

'twenty seven muskets, five corseletts and thirteen bills and sculls and every musket hath 2lbs of powder, 2lbs of shot and match as was commanded'.

There was a considerable increase in the number of cases of selling beer without a license, which suggests more people with the money to buy it; and by 1652 the corporation was operating at a profit for the bailiff Roger Gratwicke, brother of the stone throwing Sir William, had in his hands 'when all accounts taken and all made even. . . ye sum of £12 16s 7d.'

Seaford's system of local government, since its incorporation, was that of a borough and consisted of a bailiff, chosen annually from the ranks of the freemen; and some jurats appointed by the bailiff and freemen to dispense justice. The bailiff was also personally empowered to raise a townsman to the rank of freeman. As a system it worked reasonably well and changed little over the centuries. It was also wide open to corruption as became abundantly clear when the town recovered the franchise it had been forced to relinquish more than 200 years previously.

In the *Journals of the House of Commons* of February 4 1641 is the entry:

'Resolved that the town of Seaford, having sent burgesses to Parliament in former times. . . should be restored to its ancient privilege of sending burgesses.'

And send burgesses it did – among them William Pitt the Elder, later Lord Chatham, one of the greatest of English statesmen; Philip Yorke, a future Lord Chancellor; and George Canning, for the election of whom in 1826 one of Seaford's representatives, Major Augustus Frederick Ellis of the 60th Regiment of

George Canning

Infantry, was 'persuaded to accept the stewardship of the manor of East Hendred, one of the Chiltern Hundreds, and so vacate his Parliamentary seat. He soon regained it, for a few months after succeeeding Lord Liverpool as prime minister in 1827 George Canning died.

Credit, too, was reflected on the town by such members as Sir Peter Parker, Admiral of the Fleet and a patron of Nelson, and George James Agar Ellis who urged the government to start a national collection of pictures and buy the Angerstein collection of thirty eight paintings by such artists as Titian, Rubens, Reynolds and Hogarth which formed the nucleus of the National Gallery.

In the days of election by nomination there was not much in the way of democracy at work. Only the bailiff, jurats and freemen were allowed to vote and the candidates and their patrons had therefore only a handful of people to bribe with sinecure 'jobs for the boys' in Customs or the Revenue or a noble lord's household to get the result they wanted. The noble lord in Seaford's case was the Duke of Newcastle.

As Thomas Pelham-Holles, second Baron Pelham of Laughton, with vast country estates including the manors of Chyngton and Bishopstone, he had celebrated his coming of age in July 1714 with a terrific party. It cost £2,000 and the guests consumed fifteen sheep, eight bucks, seven oxen, six calves, and a large number of fowls. There were eighty dishes of sweetmeats on the top table alone, and more than 2,000 gallons of claret and an unspecified quantity of champagne and burgundy were drunk. Some months later Thomas took his seat in the House of Lords and his rise was rapid. He gave political support to George I, and the grateful king created him Duke of Newcastle in 1715. From this position of power he was to make Seaford his personal pocket borough, influencing every election from 1717 until his death in 1768 in favour of candidates who were either his relatives or friends.

The by election of 1733, caused by the elevation of the sitting member, Sir Philip York, to the House of Lords, is a typical example of what went on in constituencies all over the country before the introduction of the secret ballot. The Duke put up William Hay of Glyndebourne, a poet and philosopher and married to his cousin, Elizabeth Pelham, for the vacant seat. Hay was told by Robert Palmer, twelve times a bailiff of the borough, what was required to get a candidate elected and passed it on in a letter to his patron, Newcastle:

'Mr Palmer thinks it will be necessary to do some more than barely to give them your Grace's annual entertainment; therefore he thinks it will be proper to give a dinner to the gentlemen, a double fee to the ringers and a double portion of beer to the populace. I asked if all the voters would be invited to the dinner but he says "'tis impossible, for their wives and families and all the Rabble would come with them, which would run the thing to a monstrous expense"; but he thinks it very proper to assure the common voters of the half guinea: and indeed, my lord, I think it will be very well bestowed; for if they are not well used now, they may resent it against the general election'.

When the corporation formally chose William Hay to be a freeman of the town and nominated him as its member of Parliament the bailiff, who happened to be Charles Harison, the Duke's local political agent, solemnly read out and signed the 1729 Bribery and Corruption Act, stating he had no knowledge of any 'gratuity, award, bond or bill or note or promise of any gratuity whatsoever. . . '

At the general election the following year the corporation went through the same ritual and unanimously elected William Hay and Sir William Gage as members for Seaford.

There was more electoral chicanery in 1747. The Duke's erstwhile protegé, William Gage of Firle Place, had recently crossed into the Tory camp. So while he and his father, Lord Gage, were determined that William should continue to represent Seaford, Newcastle would have none of it and nominated William Pitt and the sitting member, William Hay.

On the eve of the election a feast was prepared at Bishopstone Place where the Pelham family entertained William Pitt and all the local gentry and influential farmers until daybreak when they were all taken in carriages to the old town hall to vote.

The Gages had canvassed and entertained the lesser householders who were, in theory, entitled to vote. They were refused the use of the Flag and Gun and other pro-Pelham inns and had to get their drinks from the Star Inn on Blatchington Hill and take them to a barn rented from the bailiff John Fletcher. He was the Duke's man and enjoying Pelham hospitality at Bishopstone Place.

When all the voters and the candidates and their sponsors had crowded into the town hall in South Street the Duke insisted on sitting next to the returning officer, Charles Harison. From this position of advantage he stared intently at every voter who stood before him and under this

The Star Inn, now part of Old Star House is in the right foreground of this 1891 view of Blatchington.

scrutiny few dared to vote against the Whig interest. The opposition objected – but was overruled. Harison also refused to accept votes from householders who did not pay the poor rate, and the opposition again objected so a query was put against these names in the ballot. When it came to the count these queried votes were declared invalid and the result was simply set out as votes cast:

William Pitt 49,	William Gage 23,
William Hay 49;	Earl of Middlesex 19.

The Pelhams arranged a sports day to celebrate and gave the 'rabble' the remains of the feast and two guineas to spend at the Old Tree or the Flag and Gun. Whereupon the Gages got up a petition objecting to the way the election was handled and it was debated in the House of Commons. William Pitt, not surprisingly, took an active part in the debate and the petition was voted out by 247 votes to ninety six.

When the Duke died the Pelham family's interest in Seaford declined. It was revived in 1784 by Thomas Pelham, the holder of several offices under the Crown. However, all the scheming, the plotting and the double dealing that brought about the return of his chosen candidates, Sir Peter Parker and Lord Nevill, in March 1784 by a majority of one, turned out to be a waste of effort. The Committee of Privileges ruled the election void as the bailiff had failed to give four clear days notice of poll. In anticipation of this decision twenty six candidates put themselves forward for election the following year, two more than the twenty four householders eligible to vote. Six, in fact, stood and the 'votes cast' result was given out as:

Henry Flood 28,	Thomas Alves 18,
Sir Lawrence Parsons 24	Sir Peter Parker 16
Sir Geoffrey Webster 19,	Sir John Henderson 14

whereupon the bailiff declared Sir Peter Parker and Sir John Henderson elected.

Surely here was an obvious ground for protest – electing those who received the lowest rather than the highest number of votes? However nothing was ever simple at a Seaford election. The petition was not against the bailiff's odd decision but questioned whether those who had voted were eligible to do so. As a result of a 1760 ruling of the House this depended on whether or not the voter was a ratepayer, a situation which led to a sort of assessment musical chairs. When there was an election in the offing householders rushed to be rated as their vote was worth a substantial bribe – far more than the few shillings they would pay in rates. In the years between elections there was a noteable increase in appeals against rate assessments

The March 1785 election was ultimately declared void, not because of the last being first or lack of rating qualification, but because the bailiff had got the votes cast figures wrong. Each of the last four candidates should have had the same number of votes.

In spite of the way in which they were elected many of Seaford's MPs did care for their constituents as well as for their county and country and their constituents cared for and respected them. William Hay, disabled and virtually a dwarf, was an honest politician and represented the town loyally for twenty two years until his death. Although George Canning represented the borough for a short time and visited it only twice, on the day of his funeral in August 1827 all the shops were closed, the blinds of private houses drawn and the church bells tolled from dawn until dark.

A painting by S H Grimm of the Cinque Port of Seaford in 1785, when it had an electorate of twenty four and still some water in its land locked haven

Another member of whom the inhabitants were proud was John Leach, Master of the Rolls, who had acquired his seat in a typically shady Seaford fashion. His 'Mr Fixit' was John Gatland, churchwarden of St Leonard's, who bought votes by renting a number of houses in the town, at no matter what cost, and re-letting them at nominal rents on condition the tenants supported his man at the ballot. He kept a meticulous record of these transactions, for example:

'Let to Mr — the house and shop, the property of Mr Thomas Sampson, late in the occupation of Stephen Eves, at the same rent, supposed to be £5 a year, for the interest of John Leach Esq. June 7th 1811.'

The Reform Act of 1832 removed Seaford's franchise and those of the other fifty five pocket boroughs and redistributed the seats among the previously unrepresented industrial centres of England such as Manchester, Birmingham and Leeds. Seaford's last two members were John Fitzgerald and pro-Reform candidate, Major William Lyon who in 1830, after a long and costly struggle, defeated the Honourable Augustus Ellis, son of Lord Seaford, by two votes.

4

ELECTING A BAILIFF – AND A MUTINY AT BLATCHINGTON
c1780-1832

It was not only Parliamentary elections that were rigged. All kinds of tricks were tried to gain control of the corporation, for it was the bailiff, jurats and freemen, in descending order of power, who decided who would represent the borough at Westminster. The bailiff was elected annually on Michaelmas Day and the occasion involved much traditional to-ing and fro-ing. The freemen, summoned by the tolling of the church bell, would assemble in the town hall and, after formal business had been conducted, they would leave the jurats behind on the bench and walk, whatever the weather, to a 'certain gatepost' near West House in Steyne Road, there to decide who was to be bailiff for the next twelve months. The object of all this outdoor activity was to make sure there was no undue magisterial influence on the voting.

A procession then formed up at the Old Tree Inn, and escorted by the sergeant at mace carrying his silver baton bearing the arms of Elizabeth I, the freemen returned to the courthouse to announce their decision.

The office of bailiff had, since the days of the Commonwealth, been held repeatedly

William Woollgar, the last Sergeant at Mace

by members of the same three families, the Harisons, the Chambers, and the Fletchers. Attempts to break the pattern appeared to have had no lasting effect although in the late eighteenth century Thomas Harben, a Lewes clockmaker turned banker made a determined effort

Thomas Harben

to have his political way with the borough. To establish residential qualifications and to impress the electorate, he moved a Georgian mansion, brick by brick, stone by stone, from the banks of the Ouse at Wellingham, to a low hill on land once covered by the waters of Seaford harbour.

Corsica Hall had been built in the 1740s by John Whitfield, a rich merchant who sold up and fled to Holland when, so it was said, a carter caught with a load of contraband Corsican wines told customs officers that he had been employed by Mr Whitfield for years to carry smuggled wines to customers in London. In 1772, when it was leased by Lord Francis Napier, the house was the scene of a shooting tragedy. A Mr Loudon, the family chaplain, was sitting at a table on which a loaded pistol had inadvertently been left when one of Lord Napier's sons, a boy of nine, picked the weapon up and aimed it the chaplain, saying: 'Shall I shoot you?' to which the reverend gentleman laughingly replied: 'Shoot on'. The child pulled the trigger and Mr Loudon fell dead upon the floor.

After the death of Lord Napier the following year no tenant could be found for the house, by then said to be haunted, and it stood empty until Thomas Harben bought it. When it was settled on its new site he named it Millburgh (alternatively Millberg or Millburg) House, for no better reason than that there had once been a mill on the hill on which it now stood, and used it as his campaign headquarters. He continued to live in Lewes, even after the bank in which he was involved failed in the financial collapse of April 1793 and he was declared bankrupt. His children must have felt the disgrace more keenly than their father for they moved out of the county. His daughter, Caroline, became matron of the school

Corsica Hall after it was rebuilt in 1823.

attended by Charlotte Bronte and the inspiration for the woman described in *Jane Eyre* as 'made up of equal parts of whalebone and iron'. And it was the tired, strained voice of a later member of Thomas Harben's family, his great great grandson Neville Chamberlain, who told the world on Sunday, September 3 1939 that a state of war existed between this country and Germany.

A state of war certainly existed between Thomas Harben and the Seaford establishment at the end of the nineteenth century. He managed to remove bailiff Launcelot Harison, successor in office to his father, Charles, from such sinecures as Supervisor of the Riding Officers, which brought him an income of £150 for no work; and Captain of the Customs House boat, for which he received a further £120. As Harison never went to sea the corporation had also to pay out £60 a year for a deputy captain.

Harben redistributed these sinecures to his own advantage then hit on the idea of creating non-resident freemen who would vote at his direction. When tried out in 1789 this electoral device caused a riot. Feelings among the rival factions ran so high that the town hall was almost torn down, as an eye witness account in the *Sussex Weekly Advertiser*, relates:

'The riot first arose from the mob assembling in a body at the steps of the Court House and preventing the entrance of the magistrates and freemen. They had seized the entrance before my arrival with the rest of the freemen. Sir Godfrey [Webster, the sitting MP], Mr Cook snr., and Mr Evans were with the mob.

Mr Cook climbed up the outside of the rails and cried out with many oaths and much violence to the mob "Down with them, pull down the rails me boys, don't let them come up". The Constable said they should all go up if they behaved peaceably, but the freemen and gentlemen should go up first. Mr Evans, the vicar, seemed to wish to fight. He challenged Captain Bate and held up his fists against the Constable and his son, who had been called by his father to aid and assist. Sir Godfrey called to the mob that he would go up but he was prevented by the Constable who desired that the magistrates might go up first. It was with great difficulty that Mr Gouldsmith and Mr Chambers could get up after they had been several times forcibly repelled by the mob. Several of the mob seemed in liquor and tore and kicked about with great force and violence'.

Mr Evans had his 'wish to fight' granted a few years later. The *Sussex Weekly Advertiser* in July 1796 reported the occurrence of: 'A warm pugilist encounter in a gravel-pit between Mr T Harben, a magistrate, in the interest of the Duke of Richmond, and two clergymen, Evans and Geere, partisans of the Pelhams . . .' The outcome of the fight is not recorded but when the votes were counted at the election of bailiff Harben's noble candidate, Prince Charles, Duke of Richmond defeated Thomas Chambers by sixteen votes to five. The Duke resigned nine months later and Robert Stone completed the term.

With the start of yet another war with France in 1793 the town's attention had turned to military matters. Thomas Harben, in spite of the collapse of his Lewes bank, determined to do his bit and raised a volunteer militia to fight Napoleon. He took the rank of captain and two years later, with his Seaford Volunteers, managed to quell the Oxford militia's mutiny at Blatchington. However, his two companies of volunteers had first to overcome a problem with their uniforms. The ones they had received from the regimental tailor gave them 'a droll appearance by the unseemly and shapeless cut of the military coat' said the *Sussex Weekly Advertiser*. They had to re-cut so that the wearers would 'carry something like the appearance of soldiers.'

Blatchington is now so much a part of Seaford that it is hard to imagine

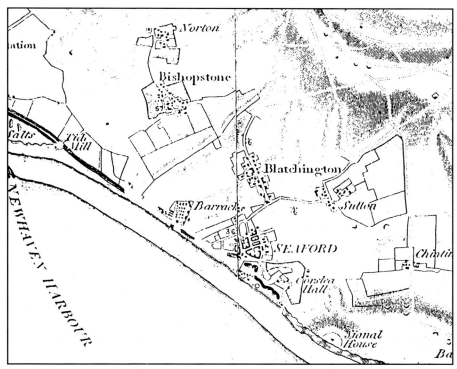

Blatchington and the barracks, on the Ordnance Survey map of 1873.

that until comparatively recently it was a separate parish with its own seaboard stretching from the Salts recreation ground to the west of Hawth valley. In 1794 work started on building extensive barracks by the ten cannon battery on Blatchington Down, just inland from the beach. It proceeded slowly and the first militia units sent to the area had to live under canvas – not a good idea in windy Seaford as men of the Wiltshire militia discovered one night when a gale blew away their tents, uniforms and bedding.

Next to arrive, to a barracks still without a cookhouse, hospital or proper roads between the huts, were men of the Somerset and Oxford militias. They were paid sixpence a day plus fourpence for food which they had to buy and cook for themselves. The situation was not improved by Seaford shopkeepers who put up their prices and supplied rotting meat and stale flour to soldiers who were there to defend them – and who each winter day had to march to and from the main training camp at Brighton. Conditions at the barracks became intolerable. The men were starving, many were ill, and they mutinied. Five hundred men of the Oxford militia marched on the town with fixed bayonets and seized all the bread, flour and meat they could find and began selling it off to their comrades at reduced prices.

Captain Harben, his volunteer troops heavily outnumbered, begged the mutineers to return to barracks and even offered to buy the food and sell it to them at even lower prices. Many cheered and agreed to go back, but the majority marched on to Tide Mills and loaded wagons stolen from a nearby farm with 200 sacks of grain and forced the sloop, *Lucy*, to take its cargo of 300 sacks of flour to Newhaven and unload into a warehouse there. They then more or less took over the port and started selling off the flour. When night fell many returned to barracks, leaving a guard of sixty men at the warehouse.

Next morning Captain Harben took over the guns at Newhaven fort and when regular troops arrived with two field pieces there was little resistance from the mutineers, many of whom were still drunk from their excesses the night before. Twenty five were marched off to the House of Correction at Lewes and the rest sent back to the barracks under guard. Two days later the Duke of Richmond, lord lieutenant of county, sat in judgement on the prisoners at Lewes. A number of them, including two local men

An early recruiting poster perhaps? An artilleryman in front of the Martello tower and Seaford Head.

who had presumably joined the mutiny out of sympathy, were sent to the assizes in Horsham; four were pardoned, one was transported to Botany Bay, two were hanged, two shot and six each received between 500 and 1,500 lashes.

At the end of 1795 the *Sussex Weekly Advertiser* informed its readers that:

'The North Fencibles or Highland Regiment commanded by Col. Woodford now occupies the above barracks which have been considerably enlarged and much improved in points of convenience since they were quitted by the ill-fated Oxford Militia'.

Five years later Blatchington barracks made a more honourable contribution to British military history. The Rifle Corps, which later became the famous Green Jackets, first came into existence in 1800 when standing orders for the new unit were prepared by Lt Col the Hon. William Stewart under the title of *'Regulations for the Rifle Corps formed at Blatchington Barracks under the command of Col Manningham'*.

And in 1809 a regiment stationed at the barracks, the 81st Foot, helped rescue the crews of the seven ships wrecked in one night in Seaford Bay. A convoy of six merchant vessels, including some which had been captured and re-captured from the French, had sailed from Plymouth on December 5 guarded by the armed sloop, *Harlequin*. Off Seaford they ran into a terrible storm from the south west and tried to anchor in the bay. But the wind was so violent, the sea so rough that one by one their cables parted and they were cast ashore and began to break up. Men of the 81st Foot linked hands in the surf to form a line towards the stricken vessels and in this way were able to grab many of crew members as they were washed off the stricken vessels. Not all of the crowd on the beach were there to assist in the rescue for this was Seaford, the home of the 'shags', and many were fighting among themselves for whatever cargo was cast up by the waves. An officer helping in the rescue had taken off his coat, in a pocket of which he put his gold watch. He never saw coat or watch again.

Thirty three sailors lost their lives that night – four from the *Weymouth*; fifteen from the Prussian ship *February*; twelve from another Prussian ship, the *Midebach*, and two from the escort vessel *Harlequin*. The crews of the brig *Traveller*, the schooner Albion, and the brig *Unice* were all saved.

East Blatchington's active army connections ended in 1818 with the

31

demolition of the barracks and the sale by auction of some of the contents, including furniture from the officers' mess, various building materials, 60 tons of coal and 930 lbs of candles. Today there is little evidence of any previous military presence in the parish. Colonel Coote Manningham's memorial in St Peter's churchyard was badly damaged in the hurricane of 1987 and has not been restored. The graves of the other forty one military personnel buried there have no headstones except for one dated '11th March 1799' and bearing the name 'E. Ward, wife of Sergeant Ward of the Derby Regiment 1811–1837.'

East Blatchington's lord of the manor, Thomas Harben, served as bailiff on just five occasions before his death in 1803, by which time the Harisons and Chambers were comfortably back in office. His only lasting memorial in Seaford was the house he brought with him which was sold by his son to another man with political ambitions, a Mr Pinder. He never found favour with the electors but a group of cottages off Church Street bore the name Pinder Square until they were demolished to make way the the police station. In 1823 Millburgh House was bought by a more successful politician, John Fitzgerald, one of the borough's last representatives at Westminster. He changed the name to The Lodge and rebuilt it, much in style it is today. It subsequently became a convalescent hospital and later Seaford College, until this school was evacuated to West Sussex in World War Two.

The coastal defences were strengthened in 1811 by Martello Tower No. 74, the largest and most westerly in a chain of similar forts built round the south east coast of England against the expected invasion by Napoleon. It was never put to the test as the French emperor chose to invade Russia instead of England, after which campaign he met Wellington at Waterloo.

Although the cannon on the gun platform could fire a 24lb ball as far as the present western mole at Newhaven harbour, grape shot or even case shot – a giant equivalent of a modern shotgun cartridge – would have been much more effective at shorter range against men crowded into small boats. Some of this shot was kept ready on the gun platform but the gunpowder for it was more dangerous and vulnerable and would be weighed and made up in canvas bag charges in the magazine deep inside the tower. There was no trigger and no sights on the cannon and it took about two minutes and a minimum of five men to reload and

A drawing of Martello Tower No 74, built at a cost of £18,000 in 1811, showing the drawbridge and the below sea level moat which could be filled with water to protect the tower from a landward attack.

aim the next shot. One would hold a piece of leather over the vent or touch hole to prevent a draught of air, while another sponged out the barrel with a wet mop on the end of a long pole or rammer to stop any still smouldering sparks igniting the next charge. This charge and shot would be rammed down to the far end and primed by a small copper tube of very fine gun powder pushed down the vent into the main charge. In Seaford winds they could not just trickle loose powder down the vent. With much heaving on ropes the gun would be run out until its muzzle was over the parapet and the platform would be traversed round on its rails, using the rings still in the walls, to aim the gun at the next target.

The 'number one' would adjust the elevation by knocking a wedge under the back of the gun and correct the aim just by looking along the line of the barrel. To fire, a portfire or slow match would be touched to the priming tube and with a deafening bang and a great cloud of acrid smoke the gun and carriage would recoil to the back of its platform. The only entrance to the tower was on the north or landward side at ground level, across the waterproof brick-lined dry moat via a drawbridge. The doorway is still there halfway up the wall, as are the channels through which ran the chains that were used to heave up the drawbridge from inside the tower. Unfortunately, when removing the original gun and carriage in the last century the tackles slipped at a critical moment and destroyed the drawbridge.

A model of the tower in section, showing its various compartments.

From a small lobby with a trapdoor in the floor a ladder led down to the lower level. There is still an iron ring in the vaulted ceiling which was used with rope and pulleys to lower or hoist up stores, powder and shot.

The lower level housed the magazine where the gunpowder was kept and measured up into the canvas charges. A dangerous area this, where the slightest spark could blow up the whole tower, so even the light was a lantern in a niche in the wall with thick glass between it and the magazine. The only metal allowed, even for the hinges on the door, was non- ferrous copper.

Anyone working in the magazine would probably have worn felt slippers rather than nailed boots, even on routine jobs when not in action. There are brick alcoves in the walls of the magazine from which blast ducts go up through the roof so that in the event of an explosion total destruction of the tower might be avoided. At the base are shallow brick cisterns to store fresh rainwater piped down from the gun level, accessible via trap doors which are still there today.

Coming back up the ladder to the living quarters at ground level there

The tower's cannon was removed in 1882 and living accommodation built on its gun platform. Today a replacement cannon points out across the bay and the restored tower is the home of Seaford Museum of Local History.

was probably a small store off the entrance lobby and the rest was divided by wooden partitions into two rooms. One was for the officer, and his room was almost as large as the second one, which was shared by the twenty four other ranks. Both rooms had an arched window embrasure facing east/west and a fireplace in the wall. The officer's fire was just for comfort but the other presumably had to be used for any cooking and water heating and would have been anything but comfortable for a number of men on a warm day.

Sanitation was primitive – just three buckets in the storeroom – washing rare, atmosphere damp, cooking greasy, lighting by hot lanterns and humanity close packed. Any whiff of powder and smoke from action above would have been a pleasant change from the constant odours from below.

5

FLOODS AND SEA DEFENCES
1800-1875

When Seaford lost its franchise for the second time many of its inhabitants lost their jobs. The rich and famous no longer had a reason to maintain country estates in the area, entertain lavishly, attend election balls and bribe the voters with cash payments and parties. Bishopstone Place was pulled down and the 203ft by 36ft barn on the Earl of Chichester's farm at Chyngton was burnt down. The destruction of the barn, the largest in the country, was just another product of the troubled times when bands of starving farmworkers, without work because of the decline in the national economy and the introduction of farm machinery, roamed the countryside venting their rage on the landowners by burning and looting their property.

Seaford was more familiar with the depredations of the sea than outbreaks of unrest among the peasantry. In 1703 the shingle bank was breached and the waves washed up Church Street as far as the church gate, flooding the wine cellars of the Plough Inn. On the morning of November 23 1824 the whole of the lower part of the town was flooded. The sea swept inland along the ancient valleys almost to Blatchington pond and washed a barge right up past Bishopstone church and nearly to the hamlet of Norton beyond. Another barge, the *Flint,* was carried over the beach and ended up alongside the New Inn in the Steyne, which was known as Le Quayside when Seaford had a harbour.

After the Reform Bill of 1832 the town retained its status as a Cinque Port and a *'Commissioners Report on the Corporation of Seaford'*, confirmed the basic terms of the 1544 Charter of Henry VIII by which the bailiff may hold court every fifteen days with jurisdiction over all kinds of actions.

In addition to the 'body corporate' of bailiff, jurats and freemen there was still a recorder, two chamberlains, a town clerk, a sergeant at mace, who doubled as town gaoler, and a constable or headborough. The chamberlains were appointed annually, collected the revenue, which amounted to about £60 from rents of corporation land, and kept the accounts. For this they received about £1 a year from the rent of the 'Hangman's Acre' which was approached along Hangman's Lane, now Saxon Lane, and was probably roughly where the car park is today.

The town clerk's salary was increased from three guineas to four guineas and the sergeant at mace, who received an annual allowance of fourteen shillings for 'an hatt', was now to have a cloak as well, but still no cash in hand. Minor offences were still tried at the quarter and petty sessions held regularly in the town hall; the more serious cases being referred to the assizes and East Sussex quarter sessions at Lewes.

'The corporation contains about two thousand acres of land and a population of about a thousand' states the report, and adds:

'The place is only a large agricultural village'.

Agricultural village indeed. In the same year that 'agricultural village' petitioned the Home Secretary, Lord Palmerston, for a new harbour to be constructed in Seaford Bay. A team of experts arrived for an on-the-spot inspection; estimated the cost of the project at a colossal £1,250,000; and that was the end of that. However, the presence of the survey team in the town had a lasting, and quite erroneous, result. The *Sussex Express* hinted heavily that a 'mystery visitor to the New Inn' in October 1845

The New Inn, renamed the Wellington.

was none other than the Duke of Wellington, victor of Waterloo and Chief of the Armed Forces, there to assess the potential of Seaford Bay as a safe anchorage. It was the only newspaper to carry the story but when the inn changed hands its name was changed to the Wellington and one of its rooms named 'the Duke's Room.' And the Wellington Hotel it remains to this day, although nothing was been found by Mrs Joan Astell, one of the founder's of Seaford's Museum of Local History, when she visited the Wellesley family archives at Stratfield Saye, to indicate that the Iron Duke had visited Seaford in 1845 or at any other time.

Another misapprehension was that the Poet Laureate, Alfred, Lord Tennyson, wrote his *Ode on the Death of the Duke of Wellington*, while staying at Seaford in the winter of 1852. A letter from the poet to his friend, Ludovic Colquhoun in Edinburgh, makes it clear that this was not so, although he may have made some later amendments to it while staying there.

Tennyson's letter is dated 'November 27th 1852' and bears the address: 'Seaford House, Seaford, Sussex.'

My dear Colquhoun,— Many thanks for your note received here where myself, wife and babe have been for some weeks and shall be till Christmas . . . I am distressed to hear of your "maiden" fit of gout tho' perhaps I ought rather to be glad. Doctors have more than once told me that a fit of gout would be the making of me. . . I trust, my dear fellow, that you will arise from your couch of torment a stronger man— nay, that ere this you are already risen for I see your date is 22 and today is 27. I am very glad too that you like my Civic Ode; it was expected of me so I wrote it. I intend to put in another passage or two if it gets another edition. Moxon gave me £200 for the first 10,000 copies which was handsome, I think.
Now goodbye and believe me
    dear Colquhoun
        Ever yours
          A. TENNYSON

Another round in the town's constant battle with the sea was in 1850 when, in an attempt to contain the damage done by the tides to the shingle bank and the drifting of the beach eastward, an artificial barrier was created by blowing down a great chunk of the cliff.

The event was well advertised by notices informing the public that 'the explosion of the mines in the cliff at Seaford will take place on Thursday, 19th September 1850 at 3 o'clock (London Railway time). . .' and more than 15,000 people turned up to watch. They rode in from the surrounding villages, walked over the Downs, came on excursion trains to the London, Brighton and South Coast Railway's station at Newhaven and from there to Seaford by whatever carriage, cart or conveyance they could hire. The bay was full of craft of all kinds, including a gunboat, *The Widgeon*, from the decks of which distinguished visitors had a grandstand view of the scene.

The operation was carried out by men from the Royal Engineers. They had tunnelled into the chalk just east of Seaford Head, and positioned charges of 11 tons of gunpowder with the aid of mirrors set up to reflect light into the shafts, for no form of flame lighting would have been safe in that situation. At 2.30pm a trumpet signalled that preparations for the explosion had started and the spectators, among them Charles Dickens, who wrote about it in the magazine *Household Words* under the apt title of *Powder and Chalk*, packed the beach behind a line of sentinels. What

A contemporary print showing the moment of explosion, and the bay full of every kind of boat.

After the big bang 'the crowds upon the beach rushed forward . . .'

happened next was described in national and regional newspapers and the *Illustrated London News*:

'At 3.10pm General Burgoyne gave the signal from the Martello Tower. . . A moment afterwards and the batteries had fulfilled their task – a low rumbling was heard and an immense mass of cliff was observed bulging outwards and then gliding slowly down into the sea. In a few minutes after the cliff had fallen the crowd upon the beach rushed forward, but a second fall of chalk when they had gone half way, halted them momentarily. Then ladies eagerly clambered up the mass of rough stones and one gentleman was observed to get his horse up on to the top of the fallen chalk.'

Seaford's big bang had cost £100, half of which came from William Catt, a mill owner of Tide Mills where storm water was seeping into the millponds and tainting the flour he produced. But the bang was too big. The 380,000 tons of chalk blown out of the cliff was reduced to powder by the force of the explosion and washed away within a fortnight.

A lot more than powdered chalk was swept away in the great storm of November 14 1875. Every south coast town has its bad weather stories but few as dramatic, or as apocryphal, as the one related by landscape and portrait photographer and local historian, William Wynter, in *Old Seaford*, published in 1922. Hens on a hayrick moved half a mile to Chyngton . . . (funny, that happened in the 1824 flood too, according to the Reverend T R Horsfield's account of it in his *History of Sussex*, published in 1835) and the Assembly Rooms billiards table retrieved from the Cuckmere (another account has it turned upside down but 'too heavy to be washed out of the window'). William Wynter says he was there and this is what happened:

'The wind, which had been blowing with great force from the south west for two or three days previously, increased on the Sunday to a hurricane. Shortly before high tide on that day, the sea broke over the beach in mountainous waves, and within a short time the water had forced its way right into the town. So sudden, indeed, was the assault that a great portion of the inhabitants were forced to abandon their household goods and flee from their houses. One old bedridden man, who lived in Church Street, had to be rescued from his bedroom window by boat. The sight in front of the town was beyond description. I well remember seeing bathing machines, boats, tables, chairs, beds and miscellaneous furniture floating about in all directions. A sailing vessel had a few days previously come ashore on the beach, and was to have been broken up but this was soon done by the waves which carried huge baulks of timber over the beach and into the town, hurling them against the houses and causing

A painting of the 1875 floods showing rescue boats on the waves in Church Street.

a great deal of damage. Many curious incidents were noticed during the flood. . . a haystack, which had been standing at Lyon's Place, was carried away by the tide and stranded at Chyngton, nearly half a mile distant, and on the top of it were a number of fowls who had taken refuge there, none the worse for their journey. At the Old Assembly Rooms a billiards table was washed out of the billiards rooms and, curious to relate, was found three or four days later washed ashore at Cuckmere but very little damaged. In fact, it was brought back, repaired, and used afterwards for some years. . .

The writer commented on 'a curious feature of the floods' – that the main breach made by the sea through the shingle bank was between the Martello tower and the East Cliff. This was the original harbour entrance and old mouth of the Ouse and 'for several days after the storm the tide ebbed and flowed through it, exposing a bed of what was clearly river soil.' The bank had been breached in the same place in the 1703 and 1824 floods.

So great was the damage and loss of property that a national relief fund was set up and more than £1,200 raised for the homeless. John Fitzgerald, Seaford's last MP and brother of the poet Edward Fitzgerald, translator of the *Rubaiyat of Omar Khayyam,* opened The Lodge (alias Corsica Hall, alias Millburgh) as an immediate temporary refuge. This kind, corpulent man, who spent rather more time on his Suffolk estate than at Seaford, was sensitive to the needs of others. When in 1858 he built almhouses in Croft Lane one of his house rules was that married couples should be allowed to remain together.

'All persons are eligible for this Charity who are of the class or denomination of labouring poor, as well male as female, married or unmarried, widowers or widows, being not less than sixty years of age, and of good character, who shall have become incapable of regular work.'

The usual practice in those days was for men and women to be accommodated in separate wings or even in separate poorhouses.

The corporation's reaction to the floods was to get a sea wall built as soon as possible. Work started in March 1876 on a wall and promenade designed by London solicitor, Leopold Goldberg and engineer Richard Creed. They were soon in difficulties, both financial and practical, and asked for the completion date to be extended by nine months. Then Creed opted out and it was left to surveyor John Lee, another Londoner, to complete the project.

Work re-started under his direction on May 1 1881 and six months later a massive concrete wall, its height, together with that of the slope of

The sea wall from Splash Point. In the foreground the work of excavating chalk to build the Causeway and other link roads to the sea wall is under way.

the parade, giving a 'margin of safety of five feet above the greatest known height ever reached by a flood wave at Seaford', was completed. It measured 3,230ft from the base of the East Cliff westward and materials for its construction were conveniently at hand – shingle from the beach mixed with lime from the works at Bopeep and Glynde was used for the wall and chalk from the cliffs nearby for the promenade.

The bath house and reading room opened by Samuel Colwell in 1811.

6

A FASHIONABLE WATERING PLACE?
*c*1800-1870

There was a population of around 1,000, a beach and three bathing machines but little else to justify the *Sussex Weekly Advertiser*, in 1812, describing Seaford as 'a fashionable watering place.' However, as the nineteenth century progressed, money and effort was spent on schemes to make it become one. A block of four boarding houses – Marine Terrace in Steyne Road – opened for business in 1840 and novelist George Meredith spent a holiday in one of them and based his short story, *The House on the Beach* on his stay there. The picture he painted of Seaford, which he called *Crikswich,* was not one likely to bring hordes of holidaymakers to the place, but it had the merit of accuracy, certainly in respect of the smell of sewerage, the Crouch and Elba (Corsica) Hall:

'Belle Vue Terrace stared out of lank glass panes without reserve, unashamed of its yellow complexion. A gaping public house, calling itself newly Hotel, fell backward a step. Villas with the titles of royalty and bloody battles claimed five feet of garden and swelled in the windows beside other villas which drew up firmly, commending to the attention a decent straightness and unintrusive decorum in preference. On an elevated meadow to the right was the Crouch. The hall of Elba nestled among weather-beaten dwarf trees further toward the cliff. Shavenness, featurelessness, emptiness, clamminess, scurfiness, formed the outward expression of a town to which people where reasonably glad to come in the summer time, for there was nothing in Crikswich to distract the naked pursuit of health. The sea tossed its renovating brine to the determinedly sniffing animal, who went to his meals with an appetite that rendering him cordially eulogistic of the place, in spite of certain frank whiffs of sewerage coming off an open deposit on the Common to mingle with the brine. . .

Soon changes were to be made, a number instigated by Dr William Tyler-Smith, a medical man from London who moved to the town, built a terrace of villas in Pelham Road, quickly got himself made a jurat and later bailiff on five occasions and set up the Seaford Improvement Committee, its stated objects being ' to provide seats for visitors, assist in improving the beach, enclosing and planting tamarisk on the green, laying out walks and providing more bathing machines . . .'

Two and a half miles of single track on a continuous embankment with cuttings through outcrops of chalk brought the first train to Seaford in 1864.

An engraving of the railway station showing the turntable and some activity in the goods yard.

It also succeeded, where others had failed, in getting the London, Brighton and South Coast Railway Company to build a branch line from Newhaven to the town.

Work started in 1863 and at midday on June 1 the following year the first train arrived, with the railway company's band on board. There to greet it was Dr Tyler-Smith, the then holder of the office of bailiff, and other county and corporation dignitaries. Ships in the bay sounded their foghorns, there were flags and bands and waiting crowds and a grand dinner at the New Inn – not yet renamed the Wellington. For the return journey the engine was swung round on a turntable so that it pushed rather than pulled the carriages back to Newhaven. The single line, which was doubled in 1904 and returned to single track in 1975, was carried for most of its two and three quarter miles on an embankment which also served as a flood barrier – an incidental advantage which became apparent in subsequent storms.

Once Seaford was linked to the outside world by rail Dr Tyler-Smith, who as it happened, owned almost all the land over which the line passed, and had built the Terminus Hotel opposite the station for the convenience of travellers, set about doing for the town what Dr Russell had done for Brighton and Dr Charles Lees Prince for Crowborough – advertising its health giving properties. He also converted the bath house and reading room on the beach into Assembly Rooms, a facility considered essential for English spa towns of the period, and had another hotel, the Bay, under construction at the time of his death in 1873.

The *Illustrated London News* paid tribute to his efforts:

'Dear old Seaford! – So good to the sick, so comforting to the weary brain, such a paradise for children . . . so calm and peaceful: for those wanting repose for body, mind and spirit, there is no place like it. . .

It is greatly owing to the late Dr Tyler-Smith of Upper Grosvenor Street, that Seaford became known as a health resort. Assured that the air was the finest he had ever known, he threw all his energies, time and talents into the place and made it known far and wide.'

Army manoeuvres brought another entrepreneur, in fact a whole family of them, to the town in 1858. Thomas Crook, a London building contractor; his brothers Josiah and Walter Upham; and his son Lewis Thomas, all had their first view of Seaford when at a summer camp with the Honourable Artillery Company, a forerunner of the Territorial Army.

Mrs Sarah Crook, a Lady Bountiful to the poor of Seaford until her death at the great age of ninety three.

Building contractor Crook so liked what he saw that two years later he bought some land and built a house right on the sea front before there was any promenade or even a sea wall. He named it Telsemaure, from the initial letters of the family's Christian names – Thomas, Elizabeth, Lewis, Sarah, Emily, Mary, Anne, Upham, Ruth and Elizabeth – and did not stint on the accommodation. It had eight bedrooms, four reception rooms, two kitchens, a play room and a large school room from which, in severe winters, Mrs Sarah Crook, a woman committed to good works, dispensed hot soup, blankets and even coal to people in need.

There were stables for the horses

One of the Sunday School parties held regularly on the lawns of Telsemaure and, below, a less formal family party on the same lawns.

with accommodation for the staff above them, and the grounds reflected the family's military, horticultural and leisure interests. There were five greenhouses, two ponds, a museum and tennis courts, the seaward side bounded by a castellated wall with towers at the corners. In the grounds there were larger than life size wooden figures of soldiers and relics recovered from ships wrecked in the bay.

Once the house was up and running Thomas Crook gave Seaford its first gas works, making sure that Telsemaure was the first house to be connected to the supply. He also bought Pigeonhouse Farm, developed it with houses and called it the Sutton Park Estate. He joined Dr Tyler-Smith's Seaford Improvement Committee, which did not greatly please the doctor who saw Seaford as a health resort and himself as its promoter, not as an holiday resort where people came to enjoy themselves.

While the gentlemen from London, the Crooks and Tyler-Smith, were competing with each other to profit from, prettify and expand Seaford the traders and townspeople, who had been looking a little enviously at growing Brighton where business was brisk and jobs plentiful, decided what they must do before the railway arrived was to enlarge the parish church to cope with the anticipated rise in population the trains would bring.

There was nothing the Victorians liked more than to get their hands on an old Saxon or Norman church and modernise it. In 1862 they set about St Leonards, removing the external staircase which led to an upper gallery, installing gas lighting, additional seating and memorial windows commemorating local worthies, including a former rector, the Reverend Thomas Evans, who in 1808 was the first minister of religion to be elected bailiff.

The church, like St Andrew's at nearby Alfriston, was originally of cruciform design with a central tower but during the Hundred Years War it was so often attacked by the French that it was left without chancel, transepts or tower and with much of its south aisle destroyed. It remained in that dilapidated state for many years until somehow, in 1485, the parishioners managed to finance the rebuilding of the south aisle; add a porch; and build a massive tower rising out of the end of the original west end of the nave. It was the worst of times for such work. Building wages had doubled since the Black Death; poor harvests had raised the cost of wheat by 74 per cent; and people were only slowly

St Leonard's church in the 1830s, before its Victorian restoration and, below a ground plan of the church showing the various periods of construction

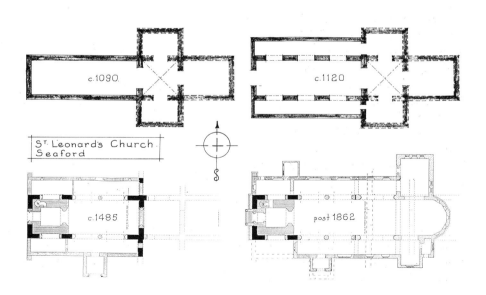

St Leonard's Church
Seaford

c.1090.

c.1120

c.1485

post 1862

51

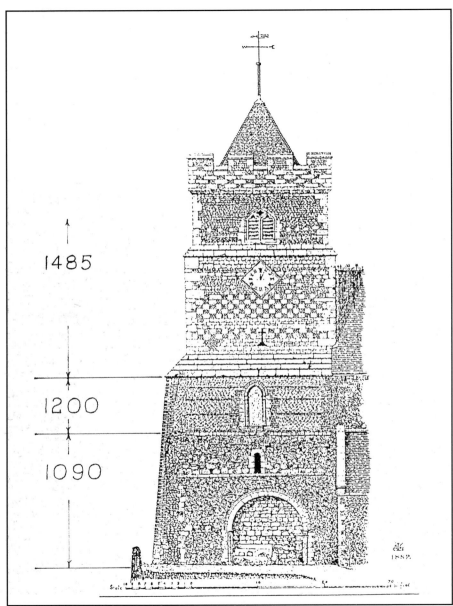

South elevation of the tower in 1882, with dates of re-building.

St Leonard's church as it is today.

moving back into the area. Admittedly the materials used were mostly salvaged from the previous attacks by the French but there were no rich patrons around to finance such architectural activity for purely ecclesiastical benefits. Could the work have been for defensive purposes? The new tower must have been a well protected vantage point in times of local strife.

When fourteenth and fifteenth century English masons were enriching the churches with the flowing Decorated and soaring Perpendicular styles St Leonards missed out. It also missed out on glorious Tudor family vaults and regretfully it does not have any richly carved Jacobean pulpits, screens or chests. In 1724 Bishop Bower visited it and reported:

'The church wants beautifying and there are some dangerous cracks and defects in the outside walls; the Bible imperfect and the common-prayerbook bad. No poor box; one chest with two locks; five bells newly cast; no chancel; no mansion house nor any sort of building belonging to the vicarage. . .'

Nothing of any significance seems to have been done until the end of the eighteenth century when a drab little chancel, of no recognisable architectural style, was added to the east end and galleries built into the west end of the nave and the north aisle. To give headroom for the galleries the aisle roofs were raised to meet the nave roof which deprived the nave of light from the clerestory windows. An external staircase was also added to give access to the galleries.

In 1807 churchwarden John Gatland, who had 'arranged' the election of his friend John Leach as MP for Seaford, decided the church's peel of five bells should be increased to eight and set about raising the money to get the work done. He had no difficulty in getting £109 16s 3d from Leach and his companion MP Charles Rose Ellis (later Lord Seaford) but donations from the parishioners only amounted to around £50 so he made up the required amount of £263 6s 3d from his own pocket.

Gatland also took the existing five bells up to the bellfounders in Whitechapel to be re-cast. They came back on June 11 1811, a fine

IN·COMMEMORATION·OF
RECASTING·THE·OLD·FIVE·BELLS
AND·INCREASING·THE·PEAL·TO·EIGHT·BELLS
ERECTED·IN·THIS·TOWER·BY·PUBLIC·SUBSCRIPTION·A.D.1807-1811.
COLLECTED·AS·A·LABOUR·OF·LOVE·BY
Mʳ·JOHN·GATLAND, CHURCHWARDEN.
BELL-FOUNDERS, MESSʳˢ·MEARS, LONDON. BELL-HANGER, Mʳ·MARKWICK, UCKFIELD.
TOTAL·COST, £ 263·6·3
THIS ·TABLET, ERECTED·A.D.1879·BY·Mʳ·WILLIAM·BANKS
GRANDSON·OF·THE·ABOVE·Mʳ·JOHN·GATLAND
W. H. MEADE·BUCK,—VICAR.
Mʳ W. BULL
Dʳ H. MUGGERIDGE } CHURCHWARDENS.

sight to behold on a waggon decorated with May blossom and drawn by a team of horses with harness bells jingling. The first set of 5,040 changes was rung on the new bells in December and the ringers given breakfast afterwards by John Gatland and a dinner at the Old Tree by their MP, John Leach.

Less fortunate with the bells was Mr George Simmons, the verger and sexton, when he went to the ringing loft one Sunday morning in 1888. He fastened the rope to the seventh bell, but did not notice that they were all up in position for ringing. He came down and placed his foot in the loop at the end of the rope and started to toll. Whereupon the bell came round with a heavy swing and he was lifted off his feet and carried up to the ceiling and down to the floor three times before his foot fell free of the loop.

He was bruised and shaken but had no broken bones, unlike his children who had, at about the same time, met with accidents which had left two of them with broken legs and a third, a girl, with a broken arm. The Simmons are survivors. A Richard Simmons and his family escaped by boat minutes before the bath house, where they were living, and the battery beside it, were swept away by the 1875 floods. Henry Simmons, three times bailiff, built the Simmons Church Institute in Crouch Lane as a memorial to his family in 1898 and gave it to the town of which 'Emma, relict of Seman' was listed as a holder of land in the twenty third year of the reign of Edward I. Another Simmons – Sam – was on hand with his rowing boat to ferry people to safety from flooded streets in 1949 . . .

❐ ❐ ❐

Engraving of a parade of the Honourable Artillery Company at Seaford in 1858 and (below) 'At Ease' during manoeuvres on the Sussex Downs.

7

NOT SO HAPPY HOLIDAYS
c1870-1900

The anticipated population increase occurred quite quickly after the arrival of the railway. Numbers had been static at under 1,000 for many years but soon shot up when the rail link made it possible for people to live in Seaford and commute to work in the capital or the growing towns of Haywards Heath and Croydon. There was also an increase in the number of holidaymakers, which both developers and traders wanted to encourage, and a petition with forty four signatures was handed to the bailiff, William Webb-Turner, asking for measures to be taken to make Seaford more attractive to visitors.

A second generation of the entrepreneurial Crook family settled in Seaford around this time. Thomas Crook's son, Lewis, had been a regular holiday visitor from the pre-rail days when it had taken him three days to drive down in his coach with his family and a maid. Later journeys were made in a private saloon which was added for him to the train from London. Lewis, an even larger than life character than his father, bought Saxon Lodge and entered wholeheartedly into the life of the town, becoming superintendent of the Sunday school and president of both the cricket and football teams. He was also wholehearted in his attachment to the Honourable Artillery Company, from which he retired with the honorary rank of major in the veterans in 1886.

Major Crook, as he liked to be known, would appear in uniform on any civic ceremonial occasion that gave him an excuse to do so. Even in mufti, as he no doubt called civilian dress, he was a noticeable figure walking along the sea front with his tame raven on his shoulder to visit his mother, Sarah Crook, at Telsemaure. He led an active outdoor life, swimming, rowing and canoeing with his children in the bay and sometimes taking them

Major Crook, here in the striped bathing costume and matching cap, boating in the bay with his family and, below left, in uniform and wearing the long service medal he received from Edward VII.

round the Head and up the Cuckmere to Litlington for tea. He enlivened the August social season with a series of one day regattas in the late 1890s and when his son, Albert, came of age the major certainly put on a show.

He had the old Congregational chapel in East Street converted into a hall for dances and stage shows, named it 'Albert Hall' and provided 400 local children with two hours of entertainment by 'Dr Seaton the famous illusionist, accompanied by the Misses Crook on the pianoforte'.

That night he gave a ball at the Bay Hotel, for 'a large and fashionable company of the principal families of the town' and the following evening a dinner for a hundred of the family's employees, tenants and their wives.

Major Crook was the penultimate bailiff of Seaford, the last being Dr Buckmaster Tuck who had set up practice in the town at the age of twenty four and was bailiff on three occasions before he died in office when only forty nine. In 1909, when his children were grown up, the major and his wife moved back to London. The people of Seaford gave them an address of appreciation and a farewell dinner at the Wellington Hotel.

It seems ironic, at a time when it had at last begun to grow in size, that Seaford should lose the municipal and judicial powers it had held as a Cinque Port from the time of the Charter granted in 1544 by Henry VIII. Go they did, in 1885, as a result of the Royal Commission on the Unreformed Corporations of England set up to review all corporations not named in the Municipal Corporation Act of 1836. The corporation affairs were handed over to a Local Government Board which in 1894 became the Seaford Urban District Council. Also handed over was the thirteenth century seal of the Cinque Port of Seaford which has the eagle of the de Aquila family coat of arms circled with the words *Sigillium Burgensium de Saffordia* (seal of the burgesses of Seaford). On the reverse is a later seal, proba-bly the one granted by the Charter of 1544. It shows a three masted sailing ship encircled with the words *Suttonii et Chyngton*. Pictured right is a later version of the reverse of the seal with the text in a mixture of English and Latin: 'With *Suttonii et Chyngton*'. The seals are on display, with other Cinque Ports regalia, in the lobby of the Downs Leisure Centre.

By 1879 Seaford had a population of 1,674 and various companies were formed with the intention of turning it into a successful seaside town. It had all the necessary main services. A drainage system had been installed in 1868 and there was a piped water supply from the waterworks some two miles inland between Norton and Denton. Thanks to Thomas Crook there was a gas supply for both street and domestic lighting.

Robert Lambe, lord of the manor of Blatchington and a town bailiff, sought and obtained permission to build the Claremont Road terraces of substantial houses on land he had bought from the estate of Dr Tyler-

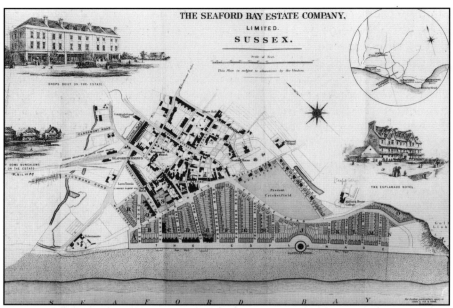

The Seaford Bay Estate Company's development plan and, below, the three of the three storey 'bungalows' built on the cricket field.

Smith to the north of the station – an area favoured by local developers, because it was some distance from the sea and protected from flooding by the railway embankment.

Altogether less practical was an application to build a 450ft long 'promenade pier, jetty and landing place, with all proper works, approaches and other conveniences connected therewith, for the embarking and landing of passengers, goods and merchandise and for other purposes' to the west of the Assembly Rooms. Not surprisingly, given the town's experiences with the fury of the sea, this came to nothing. And neither did the Brighton, Worthing and South Coast Steamship Company's 1893 application to the Board of Trade for permission to build a pier with a jetty and refreshment rooms opposite Causeway Road.

The Seaford Bay Estate Company, incorporated in July 1886, had much sounder development ideas, and more powerful and monied local people behind it. One of its principal directors was Eastbourne landowner and developer C Davis Gilbert and the secretary was Philip Lee, son of London surveyor John Swainswick Lee who had built the sea wall in 1881 and bought the disused Martello tower from the government, intending to turn it into a museum – which it did become about a century later.

The company bought a triangular area of land, with a sea frontage from Telsemaure to Splash Point, and planned to develop it as a smaller version of Regency Brighton. There were to be twelve roads running north to south from Steyne Road and College Road to the Esplanade, and a miniature Royal Crescent facing the landward side of the Martello tower. A line of twenty two bungalows, each three storeys high, was to be built on the north east side of the existing cricket field and the whole development served by a group of shops, with living accommodation above, at the junction of Pelham Road and Steyne Road.

However, only nine of the twenty two three storey bungalows were built and a handful of the seaside homes. Most of the proposed roads remained as lines on the map and the shops that were built did little trade and were later converted entirely into living accommodation. The rigour of Seaford's winters and the ferocity of its south westerly gales had not only slowed down the pace of the building work but deterred would-be buyers from moving to a place so exposed to wind and weather.

In December 1898, its coffers empty, its homes unlet, the company went into voluntary liquidation leaving behind, in splendid isolation on

**The Esplanade Hotel, with Tyler-Smith's Assembly Rooms beside it, welcomed
its first guests in 1891.**

the sea front, the Esplanade Hotel, the one prestigious building it did
complete. The hotel, proprietor G Reeves-Smith from the Aquarium in
Brighton, had opened in 1891 'replete with every nineteenth century convenience and luxury'. A grandiose five storey west wing was added three
years later in place of the diminutive Assembly Hall next to which the
hotel had been built. It had fifty bedrooms, the principal ones with sea
views and the ones at the back with 'almost as charming a view of the Golf
Links and South Downs'.

The golf links had been laid out in 1887 and stretched from Chyngton
Road across Seaford Head, with tees and holes dangerously near the cliff
edge in places. Another hazard on the Head was sheep. If they were
cropping the grass on the approach to the eighth a player must not just
shout 'Fore' and play through them. He or she, for there was a nine hole
course for the ladies, was required to find the shepherd, Reuben Russell,
and request him to remove his charges. This he would do, no doubt for a
consideration, just as his wife would cook whatever the golfers had

brought in the way of lamb chops and beef steaks for their lunches. She did so on her own stove for her cottage was used as the golf club house, until members moved first into corrugated iron huts and then to more spacious quarters.

The excitement in the 1890s, however, was an announcement by the club that Sunday play would be permitted on the links. The clergy rushed to their pulpits to denounce such desecration of the Sabbath and Anglican farmer, landowner and developer Robert Lambe declared:

> 'We don't want that class of man here who would play golf on Sundays, and as a tradesmen said to me the other day, a man who would play golf on Sunday would not be too particular whether he paid his bills or not. . .'

Shepherd Reuben Russell later became caddy master at the golf club.

The club, 'to which several hundreds of Londoners belong, many of whom occupy houses in the town, and others help regularly to swell the profits of the proprietors of the hotels and lodging houses' bowed to local opinion and left the sheep to safely graze on the Sabbath until more enlightened times.

Another body of men who were welcomed by some but disliked by others were members of the volunteer army units formed during the Napoleonic wars. Each year from 1858 they had held their annual manoeuvres on the Downs; their military bands had played on the promenade; and officers and men had brought their custom to the hotels, inns and shops and some colour to the social season. But sometimes the troops got drunk, smashed a street lamp or two and caused a disturbance. A formal complaint was made to the corporation in 1878 about 'noisy and bibulous warriors who stalked about as if they had bought Sussex . . . scared quiet visitors with camp songs and played at

Crowds were always quick to gather round any group of pierrots who dared to strut their stuff on the shingle beach.

soldiering, it must be said, neither wisely nor well.' Complaints on similar lines were made to the council almost annually until the summer camps ceased with the start of the First World War.

Respectable family holidaymakers who could not afford the Hotel Esplanade's charges of 15s-25s (75p to 125p) a day for a suite of rooms plus extras – which included meals, light, heat, baths, attendance and half crown a day for a dog – there was the less prestigious Bay Hotel, the old New Inn, now the Wellington Hotel, a small hotel up at Splash Point facing over the bay and various boarding houses of differing standards.

There was not a lot for visitors to do except patronise the bathing machines 'of the most improved style', take trips round the bay in sailing boats or hire a boat and go for a row. Organised entertainment in the form of concert parties was not encouraged. Indeed, on occasions groups of pierrots and minstrels including the Lyric Trio and its portable piano, were 'persuaded' by gangs of Seaford Bay Estate Company's most heavily muscled employees to leave their pitches on the beach. They were not even given time to go round with the hat among their audiences.

Not surprisingly, in this sort of atmosphere, the Grand Development Into a Seaside Town idea was dead by the turn of the century. There was not the demand for another resort in the twenty miles of coast between Brighton and Eastbourne and Seaford, having long lost the interest of the political Pelhams, was in no position to vie with the impetus to development given by the patronage of the late George IV or the Duke of Devonshire to its more prosperous and fashionable neighbours.

The sea front remained half developed and half derelict and the boats and bathing machines on its beach stood idle, their owners waiting for the holiday crowds which never came. . .

❐ ❐ ❐

8

IN SICKNESS AND IN HEALTH
c1900-1939

Although Seaford never developed into the major health resort envis-aged by Dr Tyler Smith the restorative properties of its sea air made it the obvious place for the country's first convalescent hospital. The idea of establishing a home where poor women discharged from hospital

could recover their strength was an example of Victorian philantro-phy at its best. And it came from unlikely source – four rich young men about town, moved by the plight of a sobbing bundle of rags they found crouched in the porch of a fine house in Piccadilly.

The woman in the rags said she had been discharged from hospital that morning and had nowhere to go. The Good Samaritans handed her over to their housekeeper and next morning sent their steward to hunt for somewhere by the sea where similar poor souls could be accommodated. At Seaford the steward found Talland, pictured left, a house on the corner of the High Street and Saxon Lane and it was bought, staffed, equipped and

The Seaside Convalescent Hospital in its purpose built premises off Crooked Lane. It closed after the war, was demolished in the 1960s, and Steyne Close and Bramber Close now occupy the site.

opened as the Seaside Convalescent Hospital in 1861. It was run on a charitable basis and took people discharged from a full hospital and gave them further rest and convalescence until they were well enough to return to the often poor conditions of their own homes. There was so much demand for its beds that it outgrew Talland and moved in 1870 to The Lodge (alias Corsica Hall, alias Millburgh) and three years later to premises built for it off Crooked Lane. Among the patrons listed on a form of appeal for donations towards an extension to provide an additional thirty beds were two princesses; three dukes, two of them the royal Dukes of Teck and Cambridge; three earls; one viscount; two duchesses; one marchioness; two countesses, one viscountess; and assorted lords and ladies. The president was the Archbishop of Canterbury. With such august patrons the appeal was successful and another wing was added in 1922.

Patients arriving at the hospital were given a list of twenty two rules and regulations and advised that 'the cheerful observation of them affects the comfort of all and assists the staff in carrying out their duties.'

Behind this elegant Edwardian facade was the Surrey Convalescent Home and, below, is the Bainbridge Holiday Home for Shop Girls.

The rules deal in the main with practical matters, for example:

2 Punctuality must be observed at meals. . .

3 Patients are expected to attend Morning Prayers at 8.15am and Evening Prayers at 9pm.

5 No talking is allowed in the Wards, after lights are out, or before the call bell rings in the morning.

10 All *Men* patients see the Doctor on *Monday* mornings. All *Women* patients see the Doctor on *Tuesday* mornings.

11 The consumption of intoxicating drink is ABSOLUTELY forbidden in or out of the Hospital, except when recommended by the Doctor.

15 Smoking is not allowed in the Dining Room, Wards, Bath Rooms or Passages.

21 ALL PATIENTS SHALL OBSERVE THE DIRECTIONS OF THE MEDICAL OFFICERS, MATRON AND NURSES.

22 Finally: Use everything with care. Keep all rooms tidy. Turn water taps right off. See that your hat, shoes, &., are kept in the proper places provided for them. Don't throw paper out of the window or about the garden.

The rules conclude with the exhortation:

BE CHEERFUL ! ! ! !
THE ROAD TO HEALTH IS PAVED WITH SMILES

The convalescent home bandwaggon began to roll and several more were set up in Seaford. The Surrey Convalescent Home, connected with the hospitals in that county, was built in 1888 on a nine acre site on the south edge of where the Buckle bypass now runs and gave its name to Surrey Road; Talland became a private nursing home; and the philanthropist Emerson Bainbridge brought a Swiss chalet from the 1900 Paris Exhibition and had it re-erected on a site between Steyne Road and Sutton Road to provide a holiday home for poor shop girls from the big cities. The Bainbridge Home was later run by the YWCA but was demolishe in the 1960s, as were the other convalescent homes, and replaced with the houses of Bainbridge Close.

The homes not only provided all-the-year round jobs but brought to the town long stay visitors likely to patronise its shops and catering establishments. They would also want something to do as their strength

The Martello tower skating rink and tea room and below houses in Sutton Park Road, part of Thomas Crook's Sutton Park Estate development on Pigeonhouse Farm.

returned, other than sit on the beach, if fine – or, if wet, stay indoors. Tom Funnell provided it.

Around the turn of the century he leased the Martello tower and bridged the moat with an old railway carriage, and turned it into a tea room. He advertised it as 'the coolest place in Seaford' and charged fivepence (2p) for a pot of tea with roll and butter. Inside the tower itself he set up a museum the main exhibit of which was a mosaic table top he had made from 20,000 fragments of wood. 'It took me thirteen years of evenings to construct it,' he would tell visitors. On the seaward side a canopy covered a section of path round the tower to form a promenade shelter and the base of the moat was concreted to serve as a roller skating rink and for band concerts.

Convalescent home patients and friends and relatives who came to visit them spread the word about the magnificence of Seaford's sea air. The writer of the skating rink postcard on the facing page informed a friend in Hounslow on February 3 1920 that: 'The sea air is doing us both untold good although I have only been here 24 hours I feel quite different'. A similar unsolicited testimonial is on the back of the postcard of Sutton Park Road, posted on August 7 1907. The writer, who was staying at Dromore, which she marked with an X, said: 'I had a pleasant journey from Victoria and the air here is delightful.'

Fortunately for the town's future at this time there was another profession as well as the medical looking to set up shop in places offering scope for fresh air and exercise. In Edwardian England the *mens sana in corpore sano* approach to education had found favour with an increasingly affluent middle class and all at once private boarding schools starting springing up around Seaford. It had everything their owners needed. Large houses to convert or land at reasonable prices on which to build; the sea, the South Downs; no fleshpots to tempt their young charges as at Brighton or Eastbourne; and London only 90 minutes away by rail. The kindly LBSC railway had even provided the station with a long platform as if in anticipation of the extra-long school specials full of small boys in short trousers, accompanied by trunks and tuck boxes.

Another possible inducement for hearty headmasters with a devotion to the game was the town's two golf courses. The 'members only'

Playing to the fifth on Seaford Head golf course.

Seaford Golf Club, founded in 1887, had moved ten years later to a new eighteen hole course 'laid out by J H Taylor to suit the requirements of the modern ball' on the Downs at Blatchington. There it had, according to a 1912 guidebook:

'an excellent all round course with no blind shots, the holes being of excellent length and variety, the shortest 130 and the longest 550 yards. . . and a modern clubhouse containing good accommodation including dining, smoking and dressing rooms for gentlemen, corresponding accommodation for ladies; and a very pleasant sitting room opening onto a loggia overlooking the last green, for the joint use of ladies and gentlemen'.

Also at Blatchington, near St Peter's church, were the five tennis courts and the several 'admirably kept' croquet lawns of the Lawn Tennis and Croquet Club. Within easy walking distance was the 'capital ground' of Seaford Cricket Club, and so was John Fitzgerald's new building estate, advertised as 'not being burdened with unreasonable restrictive covenants' and with land for sale from three and a half guineas a foot frontage.

The Seaford Links Golf Club was formed in 1907 to take over the almost circular course set out on Seaford Head, where, said a sports reporter in the *Daily Chronicle* of July 30 1904, some of the holes are 'especially sporting'.

> 'It has a Hades hole, which is excellent, and as full of danger as most others elsewhere, which go by the same uncomplimentary name. It has another where you have to cock the ball up from the tee with an iron club to a plateau high above your head, which I have heard one golfer with a gift of exaggeration liken unto pitching the ball on to the roof of your house from the doorstep.'

The name was changed to Seaford Head Golf Club in 1928 when the council purchased the Head, and with it the course.

Seaford's first academy for young gentlemen had been opened by William Bull at West House in 1866. It was washed out of there by the 1875 floods into the Gables, a former vicarage in Broad Street, and later moved to Hardwicke House.

In 1886 Colonel Frederic Walter Savage bought the Fitzgeralds' Corsica Hall (alias Millburgh House, alias The Lodge) when it came on the market at an asking price of £13,000, and moved to it the college he had founded two years previously in premises on the Esplanade. Seaford College trained 10-14 year olds for careers in the army, navy, the professions or commerce and later, as the only public school, was top of the town's educational tree until the last war when it moved first to Worthing and then to Lavington Park, Petworth, retaining its name and calling its houses there Corsica, Millburgh and Lodge.

A boy's eye view of what life was like at Seaford College was revealed in a series of books published in the 1950s by William Collins under such titles as *Jennings goes to School* and *Thanks to Jennings*. The author, Anthony Buckeridge, was a pupil there in the 1920s and used the college as a model for 'Linbury Court School' and based his hero Jennings on an eccentric contemporary of the same name. It was not until the 1980s, when revised editions of the *Jennings* books, illustrated by Rodney Stone, were published by Macmillan that the real Jennings became aware that he had been immortalised in this way.

There must have been some confusion in the post office in Broad Street which offered – 'three deliveries of letters and parcels on weekdays, 7 and 11.15am and 5pm and on Sunday one delivery of letters only, at 8am'– when Miss H M Comfort brought her girls from Beckley to premises on the sea front in 1893 and opened Seaford Ladies College. The school moved several years later to what is now East Quinton,

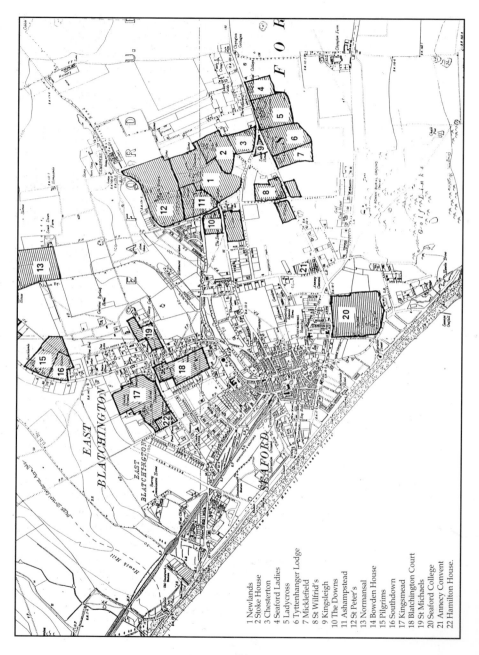

1 Newlands
2 Stoke House
3 Chesterton
4 Seaford Ladies
5 Ladycross
6 Tyttenhanger Lodge
7 Micklefield
8 St Wilfrid's
9 Kingsleigh
10 The Downs
11 Ashampstead
12 St Peter's
13 Normansal
14 Bowden House
15 Pilgrims
16 Southdown
17 Kingsmead
18 Blatchington Court
19 St Michaels
20 Seaford College
21 Annecy Convent
22 Hamilton House.

Kingsmead School and its extensive playing fields, with Hamilton House fronting onto Belgrave Road which runs diagonally left to right in the foreground.

Eastbourne Road and in the parish church there is a stained glass window 'To the glory of God and in memory of Seaford Ladies College whose members worshipped here, 1900-1950'.

Starting in 1903 with Newlands School, today still on the site it moved to in 1905, one after another private school opened in purpose-built premises on the outskirts of the still very under-developed town. By the end of the 1930s there were more than twenty of them, each with its own playing fields and full complement of young boarders and day boys receiving the healthy 'muscular Christian education' of the day.

Blatchington Court Girls' School; Sussex House (later Chesterton House School); Bowden House; Ladycross Catholic Preparatory School; Lexden House (later Normansal Preparatory School; St Wilfrids; Kingsmead and Stoke House Boys Preparatory School were all up and running by 1914 and were later joined by Tyttenhanger Lodge School, Micklefield Girls' School, Hilltop Court, Kingsleigh, The Downs, St Peter's, Ashampstead, Bowden House, Pilgrims, Southdown, St Michael's, Annecy Convent, and Hamilton House. (For a full list of schools see Appendix II on pages 112 and 113).

Top hats were part of the uniform of the boys at Hilltop Court and their efforts to maintain their dignity, and headgear, walking in crocodile along the sea front on windy days, was one of the sights of Seaford. Crocodiles of school children were a familiar sight in the 1920 and 1930s and special road signs at each end of Sutton Avenue warned motorists of their presence. An old girl of the Downs School, now the Leisure Centre, was Fanny Cradock, one of television's first cookery experts; actor Nigel Davenport made his stage debut when a pupil at St Peter's School and another St Peter's boy grew up to be Colonel H Jones, VC, the Falklands war hero.

The schools opened up new fields of employment for the town, not only on the teaching staff but ancillary and domestic staff, groundsmen, maintenance staff as well as all the bricklayers, joiners, plasterers and other trades working for the building contractors who built most of them. Also, although school uniforms and educational requisites were bought from big London stores or specialist suppliers the pupils and staff had to be fed and most of the food and domestic requirements were bought locally.

In the 1914-1918 war many young men joined the armed forces and the population was temporarily increased by a great influx of troops. They were accommodated in the North Camp, a vast hutted complex of wooden buildings in open fields north of what is now Upper Belgrave

The North Camp.

76

The South Camp from the golf links.

Road; and the South Camp, which started off a tented camp in a sea of mud on undeveloped land north of Chyngton Road running up towards Sutton Avenue and between Southdown Road and Chyngton Farm.

There were no dining halls and food had to be collected from the cookhouse and carried to the huts which leaked like sieves when it rained. It was the Blatchington barracks fiasco all over again but this time with a more scandalous – even perhaps a humorous slant. The scene that a few found laughable and many others disgraceful was of lots of naked bodies on the beach for the army had marched a party of new recruits, not yet issued with uniforms, along the promenade and ordered them to strip off and enter the water. The official excuse for giving Seaford the country's first nude bathing beach was that the weather was hot, the men needed to wash, and the bath huts at the camps were not ready for use.

A seaplane base was established at the Tide Mills and Sutton Place, the manorial home of first the Elphicks and later the Harison families, was taken over by Canadian troops. It later became Ashampstead School.

Apart from the presence of the military and the usual restrictions of

The Empire Cinema was built in Sutton Road in 1912/13. After its destruction by fire in 1939 the site was never been built on and is now a car park.

wartime, domestic life continued with some degree of normality. The camps were more for troops in transit than training units so their population was constantly changing but quite a number stayed long enough to meet and later marry local girls. Telsemaure, which was an hotel for a time after the Crooks left, became a soldiers' club and the town's pubs were well patronised. So well patronised, in fact, that on occasions they ran out of glasses and soldiers were often to be seen sitting on the pavement outside the Crown or the Plough or the Wellington drinking beer out of jam jars. That is if they were not at the cinema laughing at the antics of the Keystone Cops or funny Mr Charles Chaplin in *Making a Living,* or drooling over America's sweetheart, Mary Pickford in such silent sagas as *The Lonely Villa* or the *Violin Maker of Cremona.*

The town's first purpose built cinema, the 500-seater Empire, replaced Tom Funnell's picture house by the gasworks in Brooklyn Road where

SEAFORD

Seaford, the Princess of the South,
  (By faith so aptly christened),
To praise of thee from poet's mouth
  We frequently have listened.

A thousand pupils here at school,
  Academy and college,
'Neath heads of wise and tender rule
  May slake their thirst for knowledge.

Along the cliffs with clever net
  The keen collector chases
The butterfly; and I have met
  A botanist, in places

The busy streets, the merry throng,
  Enrapture each new comer;
Save for one awkward contretemps
  So recent as last summer;

Bathers unclothed (a shocking sight!)
  The Esplanade invaded;
The crimson blushes have not quite
  From Seaford cheeks yet faded.

Nay, turn to yonder bowling green,—
  Its players skilled yet gentle.—
Where never act nor word has been
  To morals detrimental.

And lo! when youth surveys, austere,
  His middle-aged relations,
Good Seaford calls him,—"Bring them here,
  Remote from *all* temptations!"

                    EDITH C. M. BOODLE.

Seaford – its schools, its cliffs, its sports facilities and its nude bathing – provides the inspiration for this illustrated poem published in 1927 in the first volume of the *Sussex County Magazine*.

silent films were shown to a musical accompaniment provided by Miss Chick on the piano. The Empire was built by property developer and estate agent Charles Bravery in 1912/13 and it entertained the army, and the people of Seaford, until Februry 28 1939 when it was destroyed by a fire in which Fireman Fred Mace was killed when a forty foot escape ladder from the top of which he was directing a jet of water in the flames was blown over by a high wind.

After the war the soldiers left and yet more schools arrived until the town had a semi-circular green belt of cricket pitches, tennis courts and soccer and rugby pitches. The influence of Gown on Town became particularly apparent in 1933 when plans for an aerodrome in about fifty acres of what was known as Sutton Fields became the subject of a public inquiry.

Most of the schools objected to the proposal on the grounds of noise and disturbance of the peace. Without doubt their pupils would have loved to have had aeroplanes flying over the playing fields but the schools' owners argued that the possibility of accidents and the disruption of quiet study by noise from aircraft would cancel out all the healthy advantages with which they persuaded parents to educate their offspring at Seaford. They hinted that, as the schools had a combined capital value of more than £500,000 and rateable value of £8,000, the opinions of their owners should carry much weight. And they followed it up with the threat that should the airfield be built the schools would leave the town *en masse*, removing from it a major source of employment and revenue. The aerodrome plan was turned down.

The destruction of three houses in Pelham Road in an air raid opened up this view of the Ritz cinema and the Southdown bus station. The gap is now occupied by Welbeck Court.

9

PUTTING ON THE RITZ – AND ANOTHER WAR
c1936-1956

Seaford had a population of 7,500 – and a second cinema – by 1936. The Ritz would never have been built had not the Braverys, who owned the Empire, and Mrs Isobel Langdon, who leased it, spotted a hoarding on a vacant plot at the apex of the triangle formed by Pelham Road and Dane Road, saying a new Odeon cinema was about to be built there.

Fearful of the effect of such opposition on the Empire, Victor Bravery made Mrs Langdon an offer she did not refuse.

'You persuade Oscar Deutsch not to open an Odeon and I will buy the site and build a new cinema on it for you to lease', he said.

The auditorium with its chandeliers, festoon curtains and wave motifs. Below, the flags are out in 1953 for 'the only full length film of the Coronation'.

Mrs Langdon set off for London where her late husband, Lloyd, had been a theatre manager before moving south for health reasons and leasing Seaford's Empire from Deutsch's company, Cinema Services.

'Do you think it fair to lease a cinema to us and then build a brand new one in direct opposition to it?'said Mrs Langdon to the impresario.

'No', he replied. 'My agents have been taking up site options all over the country and I was not aware that Seaford was one of them. We certainly will not proceed with that project.'

Although not an outstanding example of entertainment house Art Deco the building that went up on the site of the former town pound, last used in 1870 to house some straying horses belonging to a gipsy, did have shades of that style, particularly in its interior fittings and decoration. The 860 seats in the auditorium, which was approached through a close-carpeted inner foyer fitted with tubular steel framed chairs, were arranged in widely spaced rows in alternate colours of rose and eau de nil upholstery. The walls were painted a delicate Dubarry pink and here and there were moulded plaster reliefs of ships, waves and creatures of the deep. There was to have been a ballroom but this plan was abandoned to make room for a row of shops which Victor Bravery wanted on the site. The cinema did, however, have a restaurant with a dance floor on the first floor which could be hired for parties and private functions.

The feature film for the formal opening by Lady Elsie Shiffner on July 18 1936 was *The Amateur Gentleman* starring Douglas Fairbanks Jnr, Elissa Landi and Gordon Harker, supported by Gaumont British news and a Walt Disney cartoon. As well as distinguished guests from county and council there were plenty of patrons eager to sample the comforts of the splendid new cinema. But the cinemagoers of Seaford never had such an affection for it as they had for the cosy old Empire, which burnt down suddenly three years later.

During the war the Ritz was always full, but was not making much of a profit as there was a flat rate admission charge of sixpence (2p) for anyone in uniform. Mrs Langdon kept things going after the war with programmes which were well presented and appealed to the carriage trade which could afford her higher than usual seat prices. She died in 1961 by which time the twenty five years old building was showing its scars and was in neeed of the maintenance it was never to receive from its landlord. It lasted, opening and closing under various managements, until the curtain came down for good at the end of 1979. By the mid 1970s the only usable seats had been in the circle, the ones in the stalls were too damp, and it ended its days as a place of entertainment dirty and derelict – a cinema too large for the population it served. Since 1986 a Safeways superstore has occupied the site of the Ritz, its restaurant, its car park and its shops.

In the mid 1930s the smart new cinema had fitted the image of up-to-the-minute modernity by which the council and local traders hoped to attract more holidays visitors and potential residents. There were plans on drawing boards, but never off them and onto the ground, for more hotels on the sea front; a yacht basin in Hawth valley; a large assembly hall and car park; a seawater swimming pool; a childrens' paddling pool; a bandstand and amphitheatre; and a freshwater swimming pool with cafe and changing rooms housed in a smaller version of the De La Warr Pavilion at Bexhill.

There was to be a new road from where Hindover Road joins the Alfriston Road, running round the back of the town centre, and linking up with the Newhaven Road beyond the present Buckle bypass. . . There

Steyne Road in 1927. The New Inn had become Beard's Wellington Hotel.

were plans for a bypass from the Eastbourne road between Exceat bridge and Chyngton Lane and across Dymock farm to a roundabout on the Alfriston Road and then round Cradle Hill to another roundabout by the golf clubhouse then down through Bishopstone valley to join the Newhaven Road. . .

Britain's declaration of war on Nazi Germany on September 3 1939 put a stop to them all for the duration.

By the late summer of 1940 most of the boarding schools and civilians who did not need to stay, had been evacuated to safer places and the town had become a restricted area. There was barbed wire along the Esplanade, the beaches were mined and there were tank traps and concealed pill boxes at strategic places inland. The Cuckmere estuary was rigged up with lights which could be switched on if a raid was imminent in order to deceive the Luftwaffe pilots into believing they were over a badly blacked out Newhaven and would drop their bombs on the rural meanders of a river. The complex of buildings at the Tide Mills was used to train troops in close combat fighting and how to winkle out resistance with the use of grenades. Some of the bigger schools were commandeered by the military and on occasions the town was host to troops from overseas, among them a number of Canadian units.

Seaford was quite severely blitzed for a town of its size. The worst raid was on October 25 1942 when five high explosive bombs were dropped from an enemy plane which came in from the sea with guns blazing. The first fell on a shop in Broad Street, killing one of the occupants and injuring another; a second dropped at the junction of Sutton Road and East Street and the last three fell on homes in Vicarage Walk, killing eleven people. One

The raider scored a direct hit of 39 Vicarage Walk, killing all seven occupants.

house was completely destroyed and two others badly damaged. Another of the raider's victims was Chief Warden William Tomley, machine gunned in the chest on his way to the ARP control centre in Crouch House.

Eleven days later five women lost their lives when another low flying plane came in from the sea and bombed a group of four storey buildings in Pelham Road, reducing them to rubble.

There was a line of fire from Seaford Head to the Tide Mills on April 16, 1941 when 1,000 incendaries were dropped on the town but the fire services dealt with them so promptly that there were no casualties and only a few houses were damaged. Later in the war hundreds of flying bombs passed over the area on the way to London. Only one stopped, damaging a shed on Blatchington golf course. And one German plane, a Heinkel, was brought down in flames and this too landed on the golf course. The pilot was captured, as were members of his crew who had baled out over Cradle Hill.

The town had 1,053 air raid alerts and forty two actual incidents in

Five women lost their lives when three houses in Pelham Road were reduced to rubble.

Church Street retained its charm in spite of post-war plans to redevelop it.

which twenty three people were killed; sixteen severely injured and eighty four slightly injured. Twenty eight properties were totally destroyed and fifty four were too badly damaged to be rebuilt.

When peace came Seaford settled down to lick its wounds and cope as best it could with the austerity years of building controls, materials in short supply and bread on the ration. These difficulties, which were shared by the whole country, did not stop Seaford Urban District Council planners drawing up and discussing even more extravagant plans for the future – plans to demolish all the buildings on the Esplanade; plans to create grand architectural layouts of hotels and housing down Steyne Road; plans to demolish and redevelop much of the High Street, Clinton Place and Church Street. . .

In 1954 the sea pre-empted the plans for the Esplanade and destroyed part of it. On the night of November 26 the sea wall was breached between groynes 24 and 25, close to the junction of Claremont Road and Marine Parade, a section which had been strengthened when the western end of the wall was dealt with as a matter of urgency in 1946. An 80yd

The breach in the sea wall after the November 1954 storm and, below, the tennis courts at the Salts recreation ground under water.

Spectacular rough seas at Seaford, late 1970s.
Photo: Sussex Express

stretch of it collapsed and paving, a dwarf wall and part of the road was washed away. Nine groynes were destroyed and a number of beach huts below Marine Parade were badly damaged. At the height of the storm spray was blown 60ft to 70ft into the air and ran down the chimneys of the Eversley Hotel; slabs of concrete decking were tossed about like cards; and the Salts recreation ground flooded to a depth of 4-6ft. Scores of windows of properties on the sea front were smashed, roof tiles and tv aerials blown away and tons of shingle piled up on the promenade. The gales returned on Wednesday, December 8, causing more damage to the sea wall. A 15ft semi circular breach was carved out by the force of the water opposite the Eversley Hotel leaving a 12ft deep crater in the prom-enade which could not be reached, and filled, until the tide ebbed in the early hours of Thursday morning.

The sea had been signalling its intention to do this for years. Almost every time a south westerly gale coincided with a high tide tons of shingle

It was not unknown at stormy weekends for young drivers to come to Seaford on purpose to run the gauntlet of the waves breaking over the coast road.

The old Buckle Inn and the main A259 east-west coast road before the bypass was built in 1963.

and flying spray would be swept across the Newhaven Road from the Buckle to where it turned inland into Claremont Road. But when the 'Road Closed' notices were up not all drivers would follow the diversion signs which required them to turn off the A259 into Hill Rise, go along Grand Avenue, turn right opposite Pilgrims School into Firle Road, right again into Belgrave Road by St Peter's church, then left into Claremont Road to rejoin the A259. Much more fun to defy the elements and make a dash for it – emerging on the other side with the car soaked by salt water and with strands of seaweed hanging from the bumpers.

Tom Venus, licensee of the Buckle from 1900, never had its windows cleaned in all the fifty years he was there. 'What's the use' he told an *Evening News* reporter in 1949, 'the sea would have salted them up in seconds.' The original inn, a couple of farm cottages which became a beerhouse around 1830, was demolished in 1963 and a new tower-shaped Buckle, with all the latest design features of the day, was built next door at a cost of some £28,000. It never did the trade expected of it and is now a private house among other private houses.

❐ ❐ ❐

More new building near the sea front and The Causeway. A terrace of houses, Kingswell Court, now occupies the prepared plot in the foreground.

10

A SEA CHANGE
1960–

The private schools that had returned to Seaford after the war noticed a change. The town was expanding. Light industries were moving in and opening up job opportunities and by 1961 the population had topped 10,000. Young women who had been in the Services, the Land Army or in munitions during the war did not want to go into domestic service with its long hours and little freedom so the boarding schools found it more difficult to recruit domestic staff. Running costs were escalating with inflation and the political climate threatening the future of private education. From around 1960 the number of private schools diminished one by one until by the early 1990s only Newlands, which expanded to offer education from primary right up to A Levels, and one or two special needs schools, were left. As the schools closed down so the developers closed in for it was a time of rapid escalation in the prices of both land and property. Even if schools with extensive land were prepared to soldier on in difficult circumstances the developers probably made offers their owners could not refuse. Places with playing fields that had been home in term time to fifty or so small boys became estates of anything between fifty and a hundred houses and/or bungalows.

When all the school lands were covered housing development went on relentlessly, pushing outward nearer and nearer to the unspoilt Downs. Various public inquiries were held, objections given and countered. The big developers spared no expense and fielded a QC, counsel and junior counsel, solicitors and secretaries while the planning authority, Seaford Urban District Council, could only afford to field its own solicitor and knew that under planning laws it would be liable for heavy compensation if the developers went to appeal and won.

Seaford has precedents for this sort of thing. In 1592 Elizabeth I made a deed of gift, which is still on record, giving 'all the common land surrounding the old haven known as the Beame Lands' to the people of the town in perpetuity. A few years later a jurat, Thomas Elphick, bought the Beame Lands ostensibly to make doubly sure that they belonged to the town but it was rumoured that he had done so more for his own interests than the common weal. To counter these allegations another document was drawn up confirming that the ownership of the land was vested in the people of Seaford in perpetuity and this was signed or 'marked' by eighteen freemen. Over the centuries the land was split up and leased for grazing and other uses, but when the corporation came to an end in 1886 all the land was called in and it passed to the Local Board, then the urban district council and ultimately to Lewes District Council in whose keeping it lay undisturbed until the 1980s when a notice appeared in a national paper advertising plots of this land for development.

Seaford residents Denis Crutch and his wife, Mary, remembered their history and confirmed, by detailed research right back to the 1592 deed of gift, that the Beame Lands were the property of the people and not free for development. Although the facts were indisputable by that time work had started on site and in view of the complications and compensations involved it was deemed too late to rescind planning permission and stop the development.

Clinton Place before it lost its trees.

It was not the teenage social scene that was swinging in Seaford in the Sixties, it was the demolition mens' sledgehammers. The Gables in Broad Street; Hurdis House, home of Thomas Hurdis, vicar of St Leonards for forty years from 1733; Talland House, the country's first convalescent home; and the Old Tree Inn, scene of many pocket borough parties and political squabbles were replaced by shops, offices and supermarkets. The post office and the police station moved to Church Street, and among other victims of progress were the trees that had lined so many of the town centre streets before the war.

The Old House; Rose Cottage next to the old town hall; Stone's House; West House where Thomas Bull set up his academy for young gentlemen in 1866; Saxon Lodge, formerly Beane's House; and the thirteen century undercroft, now the Crypt Gallery, are some of the few buildings of historic interest to have survived. The oldest, the undercroft, very nearly did not. In 1954 the traders in Church Street requested its removal as it had become 'filthy, smelly, a haunt of vagrants and a disgrace to any visitor who attempts to view it.' The 27ft 3ins by 13ft 4ins subterranean chamber was concealed for centuries under a building known as the Folly, in the jumble of old cottages behind Church Street that formed Pinder Square.

94

The Crypt before it was restored, showing the vaulting.

Access to it was through a pointed arch on the north side and through a door in the east wall and down eight steps at the bottom of which was a 2ft by 3ft locker in the wall, its hinges still intact.

No one took much notice of the building, which was used as a store, until Sussex historian Mark Anthony Lower mentioned it in his *Memorials of Seaford* and suggested that it may have served some medieval religious purpose. It became known as the Crypt and the house in front of it as Crypt House. In the 1890s there was talk of its bricked up archway being opened up and the public admitted to inspect 'this most interesting pre-Reformation relic on payment of a small charge.'

Years passed, the Folly began to crumble and it was not until the hot, dry summer of 1976, when the Sussex Archeological Society's Field Unit carried out a survey of eight medieval towns in the county, Seaford among them, that the building was in the news again. It was identified as a thirteenth century vaulted undercroft of a stone and flint house likely to have been occupied originally by a merchant of means.

The Crypt in its uncared for state – the arched entrance on its north side just visible above a pile of rubbish.

The majority of the pottery found in the trenches on the nearby excavation site was of the thirteenth and fourteenth centuries and contemporary with the building of of the undercroft. The unit published its findings in the 1978 *Sussex Archeological Collections* (Vol 116) and once again Seaford appeared to lose interest in its oldest domestic building. It stood throughout the 1970s and 1980s in a corner of the West Street car park near the new police station, its future undecided – but behind the scenes there was activity.

The Seaford Museum of Local History had been set up in a caravan in 1970 and expanded six years later into West House, which was due to be demolished for a ring road that was never built. Its members campaigned for the Crypt to be restored and organised working parties to clear it of the rubbish which over the years had been 'posted' through a gap in one of the sealed off entrances. Their efforts were rewarded. English Heritage funded the Crypt's restoration and Lewes District Council furthered the museum's plans to enclose the medieval undercroft by building the Crypt Art Gallery around it. The gallery, which opened in March 1994, stages a changing programme of exhibitions and workshops throughout the year, some of them overflowing into the undercroft which makes a magical setting at Christmas for carol concerts by candlelight.

While the historians were busy in the town the conservationists were caring for the surrounding countryside. Seaford Head Local Nature Reserve was set up in 1969 and a further 24 acres of downland and the foreshore added a decade later to preserve the flora and fauna, the insects, the reptiles and the shellfish to be found there. Fulmars glide on stiff wings on the thermals round the cliffs, the Chalkhill Blue and Marbled White butterflies are seen on the golf course in summer, and occasionally the Emperor Moth. Insects in residence include the bloody nosed beetle and the dor beetle, four species of grasshopper and two bush crickets. At the foot of the cliffs there used to be cockles and periwinkles in abundance but

The cliffs at Seaford with their horizontal banding of flints in the chalk of the Cretaceous period.

The Eastbourne Road blocked by fallen trees in front of East Quinton School on the morning of October 16 1987.

overpicking has reduced the numbers.

Only a fortunate combination of circumstances saved Seaford from the sea in 1987. Had the hurricane force winds which swept across southern England in the early hours of October 16, uprooting millions of trees, tearing roofs off houses, toppling church spires, overturning vehicles, and blowing down overhead power lines come six months earlier, the low lying part of the town would have been lost.

What saved it was :

a) Southern Water's decision to go ahead with its sea defence plan.
b) The government not deferring to a later date approval and funding for the £9million scheme, and
c) the contract going to the Dutch Zanen group of companies, which did the work in half the time allowed.

The contractors were putting the finishing touches to the new beach just hours before the hurricane struck. For six months one of the largest dredgers in the world, the 439ft long *Barent Zanen,* had been blowing millions of tons of shingle, dredged up off Littlehampton, through a pipe line on the sea bed to bring the beach up to the same height as the esplanade from which it extended for fifty metres before sloping down

Building a beach. The shingle is being sprayed up from the pipeline on the left of the picture and pushed into position by the bulldozer.

The new beach makes a smooth resting place for the beam trawler *White Horse* registered in Zeebrugge when she was driven ashore at Christmas, 1989.

to the water's edge. To apply the final layer the dredger had to come close inshore and blow the shingle directly from a pipe mounted on her bow.

All the old groynes and steps were buried beneath the new beach which saved Seaford in 1987 – a bland beach, its mile-long length unbroken by breakwaters and its high tide line having little of interest cast up on it. Every so often it shifts to the east, as it has always done, and tons of shingle have to be bulldozed back into place in an operation funded for the past dozen years by the Environmental Agency.

Since the reorganisation of local government in 1974 the town which once sent two members to Parliament and had its own corporation and court, has been administered by the Seaford sub committee of the Lewes District Council. The chain of office that is worn by the chairman of that council is the one presented to the former urban district council in 1947 by Francis Coldstream in memory of his son who died on active service in India. Added to it in 1953 were the arms assigned to Seaford by the College of Arms. The design was by a former chairman, Dinah Synge, and shows the demi lions of the Federation of the Cinque Ports, the eagle of the de Aquilas and a ship from the town's thirteenth century seal. The heraldic blazoning is:

'Argent on water barry wavy a lymphad sailing to the sinister proper pennons flying gules a chief per pale of the last and or thereon to the dexter two demi-lions passant guardant gold conjoined with as many sterns of ships of the field in pale and to the sinister and eagle displayed sable.'

Now the town is to have a council of its own again no doubt the chain of office will be handed back. However, it was not to recover a piece of civic regalia that a movement started in the town in the 1980s to set up a third tier of local government – even one with the limited powers of a parish council. Seaford by then had a population considerably in excess of that of Lewes and some of its ratepayers felt that it should have a better opportunity to make its wishes known.

'What do those people in Lewes know of

'A bland beach, its mile-long length unbroken by breakwaters . . .'
Photo: Sussex Express

our problems, our needs, our interests?' were the questions often asked.

Lewes ratepayers were saying much the same thing: 'The district council does more for Seaford than it does for us.'

The first time residents were asked if they wanted Seaford to have a town council was in May 1980. They said 'No' by a majority of 610. They said 'No' again in March 1983, and in October 1987 they came up with the first 'yes' vote – 2,565 for; 1,907 against – but the district council decided that a response by only about 23 per cent of the population was not enough for any changes to be made.

In July 1988 the question was posed for a fourth time and the majority against was 638, much the same as in the first poll eight years previously. At the district council elections in May 1995 voters were balloted separately on the question and 4,634 were in favour of a town council for Seaford and 3,755 against. Since then preparations have been going on to set up the new body and on May 6 voters will elect twenty councillors, five for each of the four wards to give Seaford a council of its own again after a gap of twenty five years. The council may be new but the mace that was placed before its first mayor, Councillor Laurie Holland, at his election ceremony bears the arms of Elizabeth I and is one of the oldest in the country.

The new council will need a precept of £193,000 in its first year to run Seaford - rather more than the days of the old borough with its bailiff, jurats and freemen. Out of this amount it has, for example, to fund a shortfall of £53,000 for the close circuit television cameras that have been installed at strategic points in the town centre. And there can be no let up in its thousend year battle with the sea. Since the new beach was completed the Environmental Agency has spent in the region of £120,000 bulldozing back the tons of shingle which have been swept eastwards bythe waves. But not any more. Government cuts in 1999 reduced the agency's budget by that amount leaving the whole question of the maintenance of Seaford beach in the balance ...

APPENDIX I

DAYS OF DANGER IN SEAFORD BAY

1747-1998

Over the centuries hundreds of ships have come to grief in Seaford Bay, for in the days of sail it was a notorious trap for the unwary. Vessels would be blown inshore on strong southerly winds and be unable to tack clear. Waiting for them to the east, not with a welcome, were the Seven Sisters. Waiting on the cliffs and the beaches to the west were the Seaford 'shags', men with more interest in collecting the cargoes rather than saving the crews of wrecked vessels. And waiting around at sea were the privateers, licensed by their respective countries, England, France and Holland, to prey on each others' merchant ships. Many wrecks went unrecorded, for illicit recoverers of cargo kept quiet about what was concealed in their cupboards. Coincidentally, two of the first incidents in the bay of which there is a full record occurred in 1747 and both vessels were the victims of privateers.

MAY 1747 *St Paul*
Every detail of what happened to the *St Paul*, on passage from London to Virginia with £20,000 worth of cargo, as she was crossing Cuckmere Haven on the morning of May 21 was revealed by the rival claimants in an acrimonious legal dispute about the division of the £1,000 prize money. There was a French privateer at anchor in the bay that morning, and to save the *St Paul* from being captured by it, the Seaford Customs boat which happened to be on hand, together with several small fishing boats, took her in tow.

Their efforts to get the vessel into the safety of the Haven were defeated by wind and tide and she ran aground. As the privateer bore down on the stranded ship, her captain and crew got away in one of the towing vessels. Twenty three French sailors boarded the *St Paul* and made to

The French privateer makes off as the men of Seaford fire the cannon they had manhandled across to the cliffs at the mouth of the Cuckmere.
Oil on canvas by Francis Smitheman FRSA

re-float her but the men of Seaford counter-attacked with musket fire from the shore, and then brought in some heavier ordnance. They manhandled the cannon from the fort by the old harbour mouth across Seaford Head to the Cuckmere and opened fire. The French privateer made off, leaving the prize crew aboard the *St Paul* to be taken prisoner. The ship was eventually re-floated and continued her voyage.

NOVEMBER 1747 *Nympha Americana*

A Spanish ship captured by an English privateer off Cadiz gave the coast near Seaford its most spectacular wreck – and one of its richest ones. The *Nympha Americana* was on her way to Vera Cruz with a cargo of gold, mercury used in the refining of gold, and bales of silks and other cloth when she was boarded by the British, who sailed her in to Lisbon to arrange insurance before sending her on to London. She was on the last leg of her journey when she was caught in a November storm and totally wrecked, her hull splitting in two and the stern section ending up on the beach at Crowlink. In no time at all the Seaford 'shags' were upon her, clearing away whatever they could carry. Troops were called out to control the crowd and two of the looters were shot dead. Enough cargo was salvaged to realise £39,000 when it was auctioned at Lewes, leaving the insurers to pay £117,000 in compensation.

DECEMBER 7 1809 Seven wrecks
An account of the 'night of the seven wrecks', which involved six merchantmen and and the armed sloop of war *Harlequin* is on page 31.

FEBRUARY 1882 SS *Gannet*
On February 14 1882 the steamship *Gannet* was nearing the end of her long voyage from Calcutta when she came ashore in dense fog near the Martello tower. Her crew were taken off by breeches buoy and put up at the Bay Hotel, where one of the officers was helped by a chambermaid to dry the ship's papers which he had managed to bring ashore with him. The couple fell in love – after all it was St Valentine's day – and they were married, and she went out to India with him on his next voyage.

Fortunately the *Gannet* had landed her passengers at Southampton

Salvaging cargo from the SS *Gannet* by block and tackle. Not all of it reached the company store.

but her cargo holds were full of tea, coffee, wheat, linseed, cotton, indigo, hide and horn. A bridge was rigged up from the ship to the new sea wall and the cargo unloaded and taken to the station for onwards transmission to London. This being Seaford not all of it got there and for quite a long time local tea and coffee vendors did a poor trade.

Several attempts were made to drag the vessel clear but to no avail, and one of the towing tugs came in too close and was stranded until the next tide. After three weeks on the beach the *Gannet* was broken amidships in a gale and became a total wreck. For years her keel was visible on the sea bed at low tide and in 1913 her propeller shaft was recovered by divers and put on display on the sea front.

DECEMBER 1888 *Mary Davis*
Some of the cargo of Portland stone aboard the schooner *Mary Davis*, stayed in Seaford. The vessel was leaking so badly that she could not make Newhaven and had to run ashore near the Martello tower on Christmas Eve, 1888 where she was reduced to matchwood by the waves in less than an hour. The contractor building the Surrey Convalescent Home bought a quantity of the stone she was carrying and used it for the main stairway and landing of the home.

SEPTEMBER 1895 *Margharita*
On the night of September 19 the French steam trawler *Margharita* was spotted by an English Revenue cutter fishing within the three mile limit. As she drew in her nets to make her escape a lamp overturned and the vessel caught fire. Her crew took to the boat and rowed ashore, landing near the Esplanade Hotel, and the Margharita ran aground by the Buckle Inn and burnt out.

OCTOBER 1895 Warner lightship
It was a fine evening, with a slight breeze from the north east on October 20 1895 when a Trinity House tug with the Warner lightship in tow dropped anchor in the bay. The lightship had done years of service at the Nore sandbank at the mouth of the Thames and was being taken to Southampton to be broken up.

In the early hours of the following morning the wind backed to the south west and reached gale force, creating huge waves which broke the tow and blew the lightship shorewards. The tug sent a boat with a line in pursuit but the crew were unable to reconnect the tow, nor could they return to the tug in the heavy seas. They made for the shore and just as they were about to beach safely a wave capsized the boat and three men were drowned. The lightship drifted ashore and its crew were taken off by breeches buoy.

FEBRUARY 1899 *Peruvian*

The *Peruvian* is a vessel the people of Seaford remember for her cargo of vegetable ivory, which looked like Brazil nuts and was used for making buttons. It was scattered all over the beach when the vessel broke up a few days after being driven ashore opposite the Esplanade Hotel on February 8 1899 and was collected, carved and decorated and sold as souvenirs. The 591 ton steel hulled Danish barque was on her way to Hamburg from South America when she was driven into the bay by a south westerly gale and ran aground. Her captain, his dog and the crew were taken off by breeches buoy and for the next three days the sea was calm and it was possible to remove some of the *Peruvian's* cargo. Around 10pm on Saturday a storm came in with the tide and a large crowd saw the beached ship being torn apart by the waves, the friction of her steel plates sending showers of sparks into the air.

The *Sagatun* aground by the Martello tower and, below, the Soviet ship *Ussuri*, which ran ashore opposite the Salts in thick fog.

SEPTEMBER 24 1900 *Sagatun*

The Norwegian barque *Sagatun,* laden with timber, was unable to make the harbour at Newhaven on the morning of September 24, 1900. Her captain, his fifteen year old daughter and the crew of nine were landed safely and the *Sagatun,* stranded between the Head and the Martello tower, became a total wreck.

MAY 1936 *Ussuri*

There was an odd international incident on May 17 and 18 1936 when the 2,500 ton Soviet ship, *Ussuri*, ran aground in thick fog opposite the Salts recreation ground, knocking off a chunk of the sea wall as she did so. Before she could be towed off by her sister ship, *Perekof,* twenty of the ship's cats jumped ashore and were granted asylum by the cat lovers among the crowds that had gathered on the beach.

FEBRUARY 1972 *Walter Richter*

Another vessel that became a tourist attraction, and for much longer than the *Ussuri,* was the 430 ton German coaster *Walter Richter.* Her crew

The Walter Richter, hard aground in February 1972.

of six were brought off by breeches buoy when she was driven ashore in a gale in February 1972. She stuck fast and German tugs *Danzig* and *Hermes* failed to move her. After weeks of effort she was finally pulled off by Newhaven tugs *Meeching* and *Mallard*, with the assistance of a shore based winch.

OCTOBER 1998 *Eendracht*

Television cameras focused the eyes of the world on the Dutch sail training ship *Eendracht* when she was blown ashore by gale force winds near Tide Mills on the morning of October 21 1998 and her crew of fifty one young sailors airlifted ashore by helicopter.

The vessel, bound for Ostend in Belgium, had put into Newhaven harbour for the night and left at 8am the following morning. 'We don't know exaxctly what happened but we seemed to get stuck on a sand bank and then the engine was not working', a 22 year old crew member told reporters. 'It was quite something but we felt everything was under control and there was no panic.'

One police officer, one beached boat. The *Eendracht* waits between tides to be refloated.

Newhaven lifeboat and the tug *Meeching* tried to attach lines to the vessel in an attempt to pull her upright but this proved impossible in the raging seas. Later, crowds alerted by the television coverage of the incident packed the beach on successive days to watch attempts, when wind and tide were right, to get the *Eeendracht* on to an even keel and pull her off the beach. Success came on the third day after mechanical diggers had cleared the shingle that the waves had banked up against the vessel on the seaward side. Suddenly the ship swung upright and the Dutch tug that had a line on her took up the tow at the exactly right moment. There were cheers and tears of joy from the watchers on shore as the tall ship slipped smoothly into deep water and was towed away east across the bay. . .

☐ ☐ ☐

APPENDIX II
Schools in Seaford

Name	From to	Type
The Academy	1804-1868	Boys, boarding
Annecy Convent	1927-1950	Girls, boarding
Ashampstead	1925-1940	Boys, boarding
Blatchington Court	1880-1926	Boys, boarding
Bowden House	1907-1970	Boys, boarding
Chesterton	1910-1960	Boys, boarding
Cliff View House	1955-1983	Boys, boarding
The Downs	1921-1955	Girls, boarding
Flint House	1924-1939	Co-ed, boarding
Froebel House	1902-1920	
Gladleigh	1928-1939	Girls, boarding
Green Ladies School	1870-1924	Girls, boarding
Hamilton House	1924-1939	Boys, boarding
Hardwicke House	1904-1920	Boys
Hartfield House	1934-1939	Boys, boarding
Hill Top Court	1924-1935	Boys, boarding
Homeleigh	1908-1925	Boys, boarding
Kenwood	1924-1938	Boys, boarding
Kingsleigh	1934-1939	Boys, boarding
Kingsmead	1911-1968	Boys, boarding
Ladycross	1909-1976	Boys, boarding
Lexden House	1909-1928	Boys, boarding
Marlborough House	1930-1939	Girls, boarding
Merton House	1912-1924	Boys, boarding
~~Miss~~ Woodward's	1903-1920	
Newlands	1906-1984	Boys, boarding
Normansal	1928-1980	Boys, boarding
Pelham House	1902-1939	Girls, boarding
Pelham Place	1910-1939	
Pilgrims	1946-1975	Boys, boarding
Queens Park School	1902-1939	Girls, boarding
Ravenscroft	1910-1939	Girls, boarding
Redcroft	1904-1924	

MICKLEFIELD (handwritten annotation)

APPENDIX II
Schools in Seaford

Name	From to	Type
St Faiths	1900-1925	Girls, boarding
St Margarets	1922-1939	Girls, boarding
St Mawes	1902-1924	Boys, boarding
St Michaels	1938-	Boys, boarding
St Michaels Ladies	1914-1939	Girls, boarding
St Peters	1920-1981	Boys, boarding
St Wilfrids	1910-1981	Boys, boarding
St Winefreds	1902-1924	Girls, boarding
Seaford College	1868-1939	Boys, boarding
Seaford Ladies College	1903-1950	Girls, boarding
Southdown House	1915-1958	Boys, boarding
Southlands	1924-1938	Girls, boarding
South Lodge	1910-1939	Girls, boarding
Sutton House	1929-1934	Co-ed, boarding
Sutton Place	1947-1966	Boys, boarding
Stoke House	1912-1963	Boys, boarding
Sussex House	1906-1910	Boys, boarding
Tyttenhanger Lodge	1921-1963	Boys ,boarding
Westcliffe	1910-1960	Boys, boarding

❐ ❐ ❐

APPENDIX III

Local information

Latitude and longtitue 50 46 N 0 06 E
Ordnance Survey National Grid reference TV 4899
Area: 1,732 hectares
Population. Just under 20,800 (1998 estimate)
Early closing day. Wednesday

Tourist Information Centre, 25 Clinton Place, Seaford tel: 897426
Open Monday to Friday 9am-5pm also Saturdays 10am-5pm between Easter
Saturday and the end of October.
Police Station. Church Street, Seaford tel: 492777.
Open Monday to Friday 9am-5pm.
Post Office. Church Street. Customer help line tel: 0345 223344
Seaford Town Council, 25 Clinton Place, Seaford tel: 894870
Citizens' Advice Bureau, Church Street, Seaford tel: 896209.
Open Monday to Friday 10am-12.30pm, 1.30pm-4pm. Closed Wednesday afternoon.
East Sussex County branch library, 17 Sutton Park Road, Seaford
tel: 893420.
Open Monday, Tuesday, Thursday and Friday 9.30am-6pm, Wednesday 9.30am-
1pm, Saturday 9am-5pm. The library has on line information on local organisations,
clubs and societies.
Seaford Museum of Local History, Martello Tower, The Esplanade
tel: 898222. Postal address: c/o Seaford TIC (see above).
Open Easter to mid October, Wednesday and Saturday 2.30-4.30pm, Sundays and
bank holidays, 11am-1pm and 2.30-4.30pm. Winter opening times – Sundays and
bank holidays (not Christmas Day) 11am-1pm, 2-4pm.

TRANSPORT
British Rail. National rail inquiries tel: 0345-484950 (calls charged at
local rate)
Eastbourne bus station 01323-416416
South Coast buses 01424-433711
Community Transport bus 01273-517332
Lions Bus hire tel: 891019
Car parks. See map on page 115

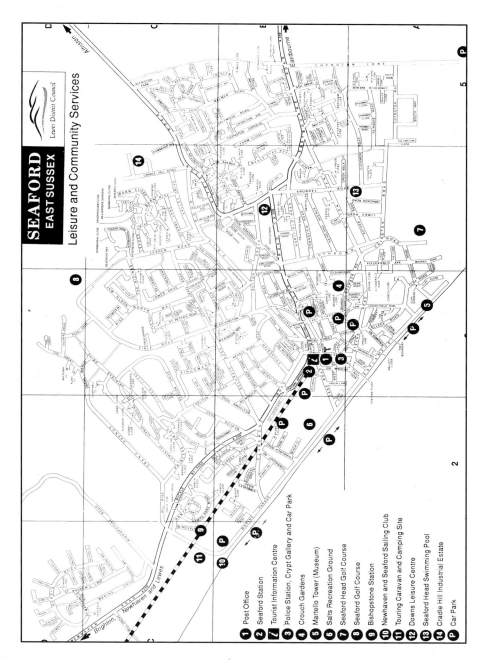

SEAFORD
EAST SUSSEX

Lewes District Council

Leisure and Community Services

1. Post Office
2. Seaford Station
3. Tourist Information Centre
4. Police Station, Crypt Gallery and Car Park
5. Crouch Gardens
6. Martello Tower (Museum)
7. Salts Recreation Ground
8. Seaford Head Golf Course
9. Seaford Golf Course
10. Bishopstone Station
11. Newhaven and Seaford Sailing Club
12. Touring Caravan and Camping Site
13. Downs Leisure Centre
14. Seaford Head Swimming Pool
15. Cradle Hill Industrial Estate
P. Car Park

BIBLIOGRAPHY

Bygone Seaford by John Odam. Phillimore and Company, 1990.

History, Antiquities and Topography of Sussex by Rev T W Horsfield, Baxter, Lewes, 1835.

Georgian Lewes by Colin Brent. Colin Brent Books, 1993

In Parliament Now Assembled by Joan Astell. J A Astell and C Rose, 1972.

Maritime Sussex by David Harries. S B Publications 1997.

Memorials of the Town, Parish and Cinque Port of Seaford by Mark Anthony Lower. J R Smith, London 1855.

Old Seaford by W R Wynter. Farncombe and Company, Lewes 1922.

Seaford and District Vols 1 and 2. Portraits in Old Picture Postcards by Patricia Berry. S B Publications 1989 and 1991.

Seaford Sussex official guide. Seaford Urban District Council 1973

Victorian and Edwardian Seaford edited by John Lowerson. Centre of Continuing Education, University of Sussex, 1975.

Sussex Archeological Collections, Vols 7, 17,42 and 118.

Newspapers and magazines

Seaford and Newhaven Gazette

Sussex County Magazine. Vols 2 ,5, 24, 26, 27

Sussex Express and County Herald

Illustrated London News

INDEX

Albert Hall 58.

Assembly Rooms 48, **62.**

Bainbridge Holiday Home for Shop Girls **68, 69.**

Bath house and reading room **45.**

Bay Hotel 48, 64.

Beame lands 93.

Bishopstone Place 21, 36.

Black Death 11.

Blatchington, mutiny at 28, barracks and battery, site of **29,** 30; Star Inn **22**; tennis courts 72.

Bravery, Charles 80; Victor 81.

Buckle, battle of 15, inn 16, **90,** 91.

Buckeridge, Anthony 73

Canning, George **19,** 20, 23

Chambers, Thomas 28

Chitting, William 12

Churches, St Leonards, Chyngton 12; St Leonards, Seaford, history and restoration of 50, **51, 52, 53;** new bells 54, 55; St Peter's, Blatchington 32; Congregational chapel 58

Chyngton 12, 17, 20, 36, barn burnt at, 36

Cinemas, the Empire **78**, 80; Ritz 81, 82, 83, 84

Cinque port, Seaford as a, 7, 9; Charter of incorporation 14; in the Hundred Years' War 11; King John visits 9; loss of Parliamentary franchise 12

Claremont Road 59

Colwell, Samuel 45

Comfort, Miss H M 73

Concert parties **64**

Corporation of Seaford, power s of 14; officers 19; elections 25; last bailiff of 58; seal and arms of 59; town hall 18; Commissioners report on 37;

Corsica Hall 26, **27,** 32, 43, 67, 73

Cradock, Fanny 76

Crook, Sarah 48, 57

Crook, Major Lewis 57, **58,** 59

Crook, Thomas, family of (see also Telsemaure), 48-50, **49**

Crypt, now the Crypt Gallery, restoration of a medieval undercroft 94, 95, 96, 97

Cuckou, Geoffrey 12

Davenport, Nigel 76

Ellis, Charles Rose (first Lord Seaford) 54; Major Augustus Frederick 19; George James Agar 20; Hon Augustus 24

Elphick, family of 17, 77,

Esplanade Hotel, **62,** 64

Evans, Rev Thomas 28, 50

Eversley Hotel 89

First World War 76-78

Fitzgerald, John 24, 32, 43, 72

Floods 36, 37, 41, **42,** 43, **88, 89,**

French raids 12, 15, 50, 54

Funnell, Tom, 71, 78

Gage, William 21

Gas works, 50

Gatland, John, 24, 54

Golf, links on Seaford Head 62, **72;** objections to Sunday play 63; new course at Blatchington 72; Seaford Links Golf Club 73

Gratwicke, family of, 17-19

INDEX

Hangman's Acre 37

Harbour, description of 7, **8**, 9; decline 11, 15, 16, **24**

Harben, Thomas **26**-28; 30, 32

Harison, Charles 21, 22

Harison, Launcelot 27

Hay, William 20, 21, 23

Holby, William 12

Honourable Artillery Company 48; on parade and manoeuvres **56**,

Hyde, Rev Robert 17

Jones, Colonel H 76

Lambe, Robert 59, 63

Langdon, Mrs Isobel 82, 83.

Leach, John, 24

Lyon, Major William 24

Maritime trade 7-9

Martello tower, description of, 32, **33, 34, 35**; skating rink and tea room **70, 71**

Meredith, George, visit by and description of Seaford 45, 46

Newcastle, Duke of 20-22.

New Inn **38**

'New Haven' 16

Nude bathing scandal 77

Old Tree Inn 17,25, 94

Ouse, ferry over 8, 9, sea outlet 7, flood plain 11, new mouth 16,

Palmer Robert, 20, 21

Parker, Sir Peter 20, 23

Parliamentary franchise, loss of 12; restoration of 19, loss of under Reform Act 24, 36

Pelham, Sir John 12; Sir Nicholas, memorial to **15**, Thomas 22

Pitt, William, later Lord Chatham 19, 21,

Plough Inn 78

Poynings, Lord Robert 12, **13**

Poynings Town 13

Railway, arrival of **46, 47**; long platform 71;

Richmond, Duke of 28

Savage, Col Frederick Walter 73

Schools 73, 75, 76, 92, site map **74;** (for full list see Appendix II, pages 112 and 113)

Sea defences, 15; 1850 cliff explosion 39, **40**, 41; new sea wall 43, **44;** new beach 87, 98, **99, 101**

Seaford Bay Estate Company, developments by **60**, 61, 64

Seaford Place, 18

Seaford Head Local Nature Reserve 97

Seaford Improvement Committee 46, 50

Seaford 'shags' 17,

Seaford Urban District Council, transfer of civic arms 100; formation of 59; development plans 84, 87.

Seaside Convalescent Hospital 66, **67;** rules and regulations, 69

Second World War, air raids **81**, **85, 86**, 87

Simmons, family of, 55

Steyne Road, **84**

Stone, Robert 28

Surrey Convalescent Home **68**, 69